Yuichi Ohta
Institute of Information Sciences and Electronics,
University of Tsukuba,
Ibaraki, 305, Japan

Knowledge-based Interpretation of Outdoor Natural Color Scenes

π

Pitman Advanced Publishing Program

BOSTON · LONDON · MELBOURNE

PITMAN PUBLISHING INC
1020 Plain Street, Marshfield, Massachusetts 02050

PITMAN PUBLISHING LIMITED
128 Long Acre, London WC2E 9AN

Associated Companies
Pitman Publishing Pty Ltd, Melbourne
Pitman Publishing New Zealand Ltd, Wellington
Copp Clark Pitman, Toronto

First published 1985

Library of Congress Cataloging in Publication Data

Ohta, Yuichi, 1949
    Knowledge-based interpretation of outdoor natural
    color scenes.
    'Pitman advanced publishing program.'
    Bibliography: p.
    Includes index.
    1. Image processing.   2. Color.   3. Artificial
intelligence.   I. Title
    TA1632.058   1985   001.53'4   84-26562

ISBN 0-273-08673-1

British Library Cataloguing in Publication Data

Ohta, Yuichi
    Knowledge-based interpretation of outdoor
    natural color scenes.—(Research notes in artificial intelligence; v. 4)
    1. Optical pattern recognition
    I. Title   II. Series
    001.5'34   TA1650

ISBN 0-273-08673-1

Reproduced and printed by photolithography
in Great Britain by Biddles Ltd, Guildford

Knowledge-based Interpreta
of Outdoor Natural
Color Scenes

012171094

Contents

Preface

In this paper, a region analyzer for outdoor natural color scenes is studied. The major issues addressed and described here are the following: (1) the role of color information in region segmentation; (2) the technique of partitioning an image into a set of regions; (3) the technique of managing the regions in a symbolic data structure; and (4) the modeling and control scheme for obtaining the "best" match between the model of a task world and the set of regions obtained from an input image.

Systematic experiments have been performed to examine the role of color information in region segmentation. A segmentation scheme, called the "dynamic K-L transformation", was developed for this purpose. A new set of color features effective for region segmentation was found.

A powerful segmentation program was developed for preliminarily partitioning an image data into a set of regions. The result of segmentation was organized into a well-structured symbolic data network, called the "Patchery Data Structure", with various retrieval facilities.

The knowledge of the task world was represented as a set of rules. Bottom-up control and top-down control were combined in the rule-based region analyzer. A plan was generated by the bottom-up control as the representation of coarse structures in the input scene. A symbolic description of the scene was made in the top-down analysis. The top-down process was implemented by using a production system architecture.

Outdoor scenes including sky, trees, buildings, and roads have been successfully analyzed by the system.

This paper is a revised version of a doctorial thesis which was submitted in partial fulfillment of the requirements for the degree of Doctor of Engineering at tne Department of Information Science, Kyoto University. The original title was "A region-oriented image-analysis system by computer".

Yuichi Ohta

Acknowledgements

The work described herein was done at the Department of Information Science, Kyoto University.

I would like to express my sincere appreciation to Professor Toshiyuki Sakai of Kyoto University for supervising this research with adequate guidance and constant encouragement.

I am also grateful to Associate Professor Takeo Kanade of Carnegie-Mellon University, who was originally at Kyoto University, for introducing me to this field. He gave me continuing advice and had enlightening discussions with me.

Finally, thanks go to my wife, Kiyomi, for her help in many ways. Cheerful encouragement given by my son, Yusuke, and daughter, Mariko, should be noted here.

Yuichi Ohta

1 Introduction

An image is a two-dimensional (2-D) projection of a three-dimensional (3-D) scene. The task of an image analysis system is to make a description of the scene from its image. A complete 3-D description of the scene, of course, cannot be reconstructed from the image data alone, since the information contained in an image is not sufficient to determine all the "parameters" necessary for the description.

In order to make the problem actually solvable, the number of parameters should be reduced. One way to do this is to restrict the class of scenes to which the image analysis system is applied. Such a restricted world is called a "task". Within the task world, it is possible to find a set of "rewriting rules" which map image features into scene description. These rewriting rules are called the "knowledge" of the task world and they are represented in the model.

In this paper, a scheme for model representation and a control structure for image analysis are examined in detail. As well as the "higher level" problems dealing with representation and use of knowledge, much attention is paid to the "lower level" ones, such as signal-based region segmentation or representation of segmented regions.

A region analysis method is employed to organize our image analysis system. Region analysis and edge analysis are two of the major methods employed in analyzing pictures; regions and edges are complementary to each other. Yet, region analysis has not been studied as much as edge analysis. Recently, region analysis techniques have been capturing attention for several reasons. One of the most significant reasons is that some problems can be solved more easily by using regions than by using edges.

This paper describes a region analyzer for natural color scenes. The primary task to which the analyzer has been applied is outdoor scenes. This is because outdoor scenes include such objects as trees, sky, etc., which are naturally defined by the properties of regions rather than of edges. The placement relations among the objects can be dealt with easily by using regions. The major issues addressed and described in this paper are the following: (1) the role of color information in region segmentation; (2) the technique of

1

partitioning an image into a set of regions; (3) the technique of managing the regions in a symbolic data structure; and (4) the modeling and control scheme for obtaining the "best" match between the model of a task world and the set of regions obtained from an input image.

1.1. Aspects of Region Analysis

A region analysis system covers a wide range of subjects varying from the digitization of pictures to their semantic interpretation. In this paper, we assume that an input color image is given as a set of digitized intensity arrays corresponding to the red, green, and blue components of color.

Color information for region segmentation   The subject of color image segmentation might be studied as a simple extension of segmentation for black and white images. Many researchers have recognized the importance of color information in image segmentation. However, how effectively one can use chromatic information in the segmentation process and what color coordinate systems are most appropriate have not been much studied. We have tried to obtain a solution for these problems in the case of region segmentation. A set of color features is derived through an experiment of computing effective color features by means of the Karhunen-Loeve transformation at every step of segmenting a region. Comparisons are made among the segmentation results obtained by using the various sets of color features which are usually used in image analysis. This is one of the first systematic experiments actually performed to find the effective color information in segmentation. Chapter 2 describes this issue in detail.

Region segmentation technique   Region segmentation is a process which partitions an image into a set of regions. Each region is characterized by some consistent features such as color or texture, and such regions are often called "coherent" or "homogeneous" regions. Regions in an image correspond to surfaces of objects in a real world. Region segmentation is thus based on the assumption that characteristics of a surface are usually consistent. The coherent regions are not always equal to meaningful regions in many cases, but they are the atomic elements for constructing a description of the scene.

Region segmentation techniques can be divided into three classes: (1) region splitting, (2) region merging, and (3) combined use of splitting and merging.

2

The region splitting technique partitions an image into regions in a top-to-bottom manner. It starts with the entire image and works toward the set of "coherent" regions. The distribution of image features in the spectral domain is often used to obtain criteria for the splitting operation [Tomita et al., 1973; Ohlander, 1975]. The method often works well for extracting global structures in the image, but is weak for detecting detailed ones.

The region segmentation technique based on region merging operations is alternatively called region growing. It starts with atomic regions, e.g., pixels or tiny square regions, and works toward the set of "coherent" regions in a bottom-to-top manner. Local spatial features, such as the contrast at boundaries between regions, are used as criteria for the merging operation [Brice et al., 1970]. The method is good in extracting detailed structures in the image, but is rather sensitive to noise.

The spatial resolution of segmented regions can be defined as the ratio of the size of the atomic region to that of the whole image. Region growing usually requires far more computation than does region splitting to achieve the same spatial resolution.

The split-and-merge method [Horowitz and Pavlidis, 1974] aims to gain computational efficiency by preserving the merits of both the splitting and the merging methods. A pyramidal data structure [Tanimoto and Pavlidis, 1975] provides a working environment for this method [Pavlidis, 1979].

If the regions are used as atomic elements for image analysis, they must have sufficient spatial resolution to evaluate shape parameters of objects. There are many algorithms for obtaining a set of regions, but actually only a few algorithms can produce a segmentation of an image with satisfactory resolution. The segmentation algorithm developed in our system is of the splitting type. It can extract the detailed structures in the image as well as the global ones with sufficient spatial resolution. Chapter 3 describes this issue.

Symbolic representation of regions   A region segmentation process produces as a result a two-dimensional array which indicates the region numbers: the points in the same region have the same number. Any data about the segmented image can be derived from this array and the original image. The computation needed for the derivation, however, is time consuming, because it must deal with the image arrays directly.

When regions rather than pixels are used as atomic elements for analysis, one can perform the analysis without dealing with the two-dimensional image arrays at all. The data needed for the analysis can be described by using the regions as descriptive elements. In order to support the high-speed retrieval of any kind of data about the segmented image, the description should be a well-organized data structure. Data retrieval facilities for the data structure are also essential to enable the flexible retrieval of pictorial data.

A structured data network, called the "Patchery Data Structure", is defined together with a set of retrieval functions. Regions, boundary segments, vertices, etc. are used as the descriptive elements. This subject is also described in chapter 3.

Modeling and control for region analysis   The model in an image analysis system represents the knowledge of the world in which the system works. Objects and various concepts are defined in the model by using terms which correspond to the real world. But it must be noted that the knowledge in the model is valid only in the restricted world which is given as a task. That is, the objects and the various concepts in the model are defined within the restricted task world, and they are not always usable in the unrestricted real world.

It is well known that there are two complementary methods for model representation: procedural and declarative.

In the procedural method, the knowledge is embedded in the program which performs the image analysis. The control structure of the method is defined implicitly in the control of the program. Given a task, the procedural method provides a flexible scheme for constructing an efficient image analysis system. But the structure of the analysis mechanism is rather unclear, and a slight change in the task often demands complete changes in the system. A successful example of the procedural method can be found in the face-analysis program developed by Kanade [Sakai et al., 1972; Kanade, 1977].,

In the declarative method, the model is represented as a collection of descriptions of properties of, or relations between, the objects. The model has a modular structure and the control structure is clear. However, it is very difficult to develop a modeling and control scheme in a declarative fashion when the task world is complex.

Recently, rule-based architectures such as production systems [Davis and King, 1975] have been employed to construct expert systems in Artificial Intelligence. In these architectures, the model is represented as a collection

4

of simple modules, and the control structure is also simple. They aim to combine the merits of both the procedural and declarative methods. The work described in this paper employs a rule-based architecture in region analysis.

The control structure in an image analysis system defines the way to search for the "best" match between a model and an input image. In region analysis, the input image is first partitioned into a set of "coherent" regions based on intensity information. If the coherent regions are in one-to-one correspondence with the objects defined in the model, i.e., the coherent regions are the meaningful ones, then it is an easy problem to search for the "best" match between the regions and the objects. It is almost impossible, however, to obtain a set of meaningful regions by using only the "low-level" image information (i.e. intensity or color), and the control structure must search for a many-to-one correspondence between the regions and the objects.

The depth of the search tree in the image interpretation is determined by the number of regions. Tne branching factor is determined by the number of objects. The search space is prohibitively large, but the situation is a little better than the ordinary search tree in game problems, since scenes have a favorable property which may be called "locality". By applying this property to the search scheme, it is possible to reduce the search space drastically.

The details of our modeling and control scheme are described in chapter 4.

1.2. Overview of the Region Analyzer

This section provides the reader with an outline of the region analyzer which is developed in this paper. The main issues and the detailed descriptions will be included in the following chapters. Figure 1-1 shows two major steps of the analysis mechanism: the preliminary segmentation and the rule-based analysis. The system receives red-green-blue intensity arrays of a digitized image and constructs a semantic description of the scene.

Preliminary segmentation --- This step is basically "nonpurposive", and it can be applied to a wide range of tasks. The primary objective of the preliminary segmentation is not the reduction but the structuring of raw image data into usable information. It segments the input color image into a set of coherent regions based on the color information. An Ohlander-type segmentation algorithm [Ohlander, 1975] is employed with several improvements to extract detailed structures from the image data. The regions obtained by the preliminary segmentation are used as the atomic

5

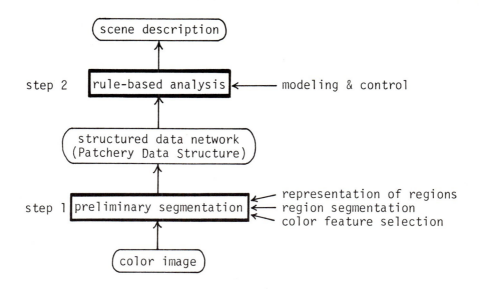

Figure 1-1.   Two steps in region analysis; from an input
             color image to the scene description.

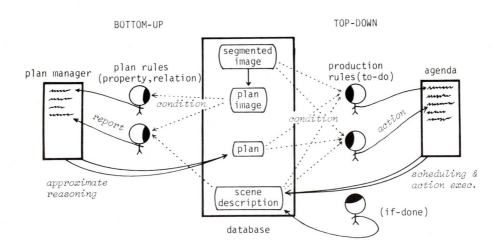

Figure 1-2.   Schematic diagram of the rule-based analysis.

6

elements to construct the description of the scene. They are organized into a fully-structured symbolic data network, called the "Patchery Data Structure", with powerful retrieval facilities. In the rule-based analysis, all picture-processing operations are performed on this Patchery Data Structure rather than the raw image data. This enables the rule-based analysis to have a clear-cut scheme for modeling and control, and to perform various picture processing operations efficiently.

Rule-based analysis --- Figure 1-2 shows the schematic diagram of the rule-based architecture in our system. It employs both bottom-up and top-down control schemes. Knowledge of the task world is represented by two sets of rules: one is for the bottom-up process and the other for the top-down process. The rules for the bottom-up process make a plan as a rough interpretation of the scene. The rules for the top-down process make a detailed semantic description of the scene.

An approximate reasoning scheme is employed for plan evaluation to deal with the uncertainty which exists in both knowledge and pictorial features. The plan manager controls the evaluation of plan.

The top-down analysis works in the framework of region growing. But the process is not a simple iteration of the labeling and merging operations. A scene description is built as the result of the top-down analysis. The knowledge used in the top-down process is represented as a set of production rules. An agenda controls the production system. Each production rule is a condition-action pair, where the "condition" is a fuzzy predicate [Lee and Chang, 1971]. It checks the state of the database and decides whether the associated action can be executed. Each "action" describes the operations needed to build the scene description. Every executable action is given a score to indicate its priority and is registered on the agenda. The action with the highest score is executed at each stage of analysis, and as a result the database is changed. Production rules are activated again to examine the database. In order to reduce the computation, the agenda controls the activation of production rules according to the changes newly made in the database.

The analysis process completes when all regions are interpreted and assembled into the scene description.

1.3. Related Work

In this section, a brief survey of analysis systems for natural scenes is presented. Only complete systems are referred to here. The work relating to individual problems such as color representation, segmentation, and region analysis is mentioned in the corresponding chapters. A survey of region analysis techniques in general can be found elsewhere [Kanade, 1978].

a) Barrow and Popplestone [1971] constructed a system which interprets isolated simple objects, such as cup, spectacles, cylinder, etc. The image data is first partitioned into a set of regions. The set of regions is then described in the form of a graph which represents properties of and relations between the regions. The description is matched against a set of models which describe typical views of objects. A limitation of this work is that it requires the regions to be meaningful ones. However, it is very difficult to obtain meaningful partitions based only on pictorial features.

b) Preparata and Ray [1972] tried to interpret simple outdoor scenes by using a graph matching scheme similar to that of Barrow and Popplestone. In their work, the image was manually partitioned into regions to avoid difficulties in the automatic region segmentation.

c) Yakimovsky and Feldman [1973] integrated the segmentation and interpretation phases. The input image was first segmented into coherent regions. Object labels were assigned to each region by using knowledge of the task world, and those regions which were assigned the same labels were merged. The knowledge was represented by a set of probabilities. The interpretation was performed by maximizing the joint probability that regions have correct labels. They successfully analyzed road scenes and X-ray images.

d) Tenenbaum and Barrow [1976] developed a scheme called Interpretation-Guided Segmentation to integrate the segmentation and interpretation phases. In their case, the knowledge was represented as a set of constraints and Waltz's filtering algorithm [Waltz, 1975] was employed to search for a globally correct interpretation.

8

e) Rubin and Reddy [1977] represented the task knowledge in the form of a pixel-level constraint network. All images that are admissible in a task world were precompiled into the network. Given an input image, the system searched through the network for a path corresponding to the "best" match between the model and the image data.

f) Bajcsy and Lieberman [1974] analyzed simple outdoor scenes by using a top-down control structure. The knowledge was embedded in the procedures which extract objects from image data.

g) Sloan [1977] employed a production system architecture to represent the knowledge of outdoor scenes. Each production rule was triggered by a certain pictorial feature. It simply rephrased the facts recorded in the database or tried to extract some objects from the image data in a top-down fashion.

h) Freuder [1977] represented the knowledge by a set of modular procedures ana organized them into a semantic network. Each module had its own duty and it activated other modules when necessary. A simple "hammer" scene was used as the task world.

i) Riseman et al. [1977] tried to construct a scene analysis system named VISIONS. The knowledge was represented in a hierarchical structure with layers, such as objects, volumes, surfaces, regions, etc. At each level of the hierarchy, a hypothesis-and-test paradigm was used to construct a scene description from the image data.

There are two complementary control schemes, bottom-up and top-down, to organize a scene analysis system. One can categorize the systems described above into two groups: a) through e) employ the bottom-up scheme, and f) through i) the top-down. The first group relies on a bottom-up control structure together with global optimization mechanisms. On the other hand, the second group utilizes a top-down control scheme with or without a bottom-up mechanism to trigger the top-down scheme. Notice that a mechanism to search for a globally (sub)optimal solution is included in the first group, whereas the second group takes a solution found first in a depth-first search. The system described in this paper employs both the top-down control and bottom-up control schemes together with optimizing mechanisms. It aims to combine the merits of the two complementary control schemes.

2 Color Information for Region Segmentation

2.1. The Problems

In color image processing, the color of a pixel is usually given as three values corresponding to the tristimulus values R (red), G (green), and B (blue). Various kinds of color features, such as intensity (D), saturation (S), and hue (H), can be calculated from {R, G, B} by using either linear or nonlinear transformations. Each color feature has its own characteristics. For instance, the set {D, S, H} is convenient for representing human color perception; the set {Y, I, Q} is used to efficiently encode color information in TV signals; and the normalized color set {r, g, b} is convenient for representing the color plane.

It seems that in computer processing of color images, color features which were developed for other purposes have been used in different combinations for different purposes. Nevatia [1976] extended the Hueckel operator for color edge extraction. He stated that the result obtained using intensity (D=R+G+B) and normalized colors (r=R/D and g=G/D) was better than that obtained using R, G, and B. Ohlander [1975] employed nine redundant color features R, G, B, Y, I, Q, D, S, and H for color image segmentation. He reported that H was most useful and that Y, I, and Q were rarely used.

Kender [1976] presented a very careful discussion of the behavior of the linear and nonlinear color transformations used to obtain color features such as hue, saturation, and normalized color from R, G, and B. His discussion amounts to two points: (1) Nonlinear transformations such as hue, saturation, and normalized color have nonremovable singularities, near which a small perturbation of the input R, G, and B can cause a large jump in the transformed values; (2) the distribution of the nonlinearly transformed values can show spurious modes and gaps. For these reasons and from the computational point of view, he concluded that linear transformations such as Y, I, and Q are preferable to nonlinear ones.

It is an interesting and important problem to find color features which are suited for the segmentation of color images by computer. One way to get such color features is to perform the segmentation by using various sets of color features and to compare the results. However, this allows us to examine only predefined sets of color features. In this chapter we attempt to derive a set of effective color features by systematic experiments in region segmentation. An Ohlander-type segmentation algorithm by recursive thresholding is employed as a tool for the experiments. At each step of segmenting a region, new color features are calculated for the pixels in that region by the Karhunen-Loeve transformation of the R, G, and B data. By analyzing the color features obtained in segmenting eight kinds of color pictures, we have found a set of effective color features. The effectiveness of our color feature set is shown by a comparative study with various other sets of color features which are commonly used in image analysis.

2.2. Selection of Effective Color Features

2.2.1. Segmentation algorithm

First of all, the segmentation algorithm which was employed in the experiments will be briefly described. The basic scheme is almost the same as the segmentation algorithm described in chapter 3. Figure 2-1 shows a schematic diagram of the segmentation algorithm. The basic idea of the process is as follows: The whole image is first partitioned into sub-images each of which is a connected region; then each sub-image is further partitioned if possible; and this process iterates. Because of the recursive nature of the algorithm, a picture stack is used to store the region masks. A region mask represents a connected region (the area without hatching in figure 2-1) which is to be examined for segmentation. The arrows with numbers shown in figure 2-1 represent the following operations.

(0) A mask corresponding to the whole image is placed at the bottom of the stack.
(1) One mask is taken from the top of the stack. Let S denote the region represented by the mask (the area without hatching).
(2) Histograms of color features in the region S are computed.
(3) If any of the histograms shows conspicuous peaks, a pair of cutoff values which separate the peak in the histogram are determined at the position of valleys, and the image of the color feature corresponding to that histogram is thresholded using the cutoff values; thus the region S is partitioned. Otherwise, region S is not partitioned further.

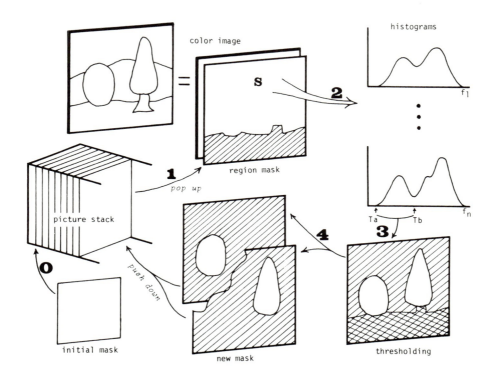

Figure 2-1. Schematic diagram of the segmentation algorithm.

13

(4) Connected regions are extracted. For each connected region, a region mask
     is generated, and it is pushed down on the stack.

Operations (1)-(4) are iterated until the picture stack becomes empty. In
operation (3), the cutoff values are selected by the following two criteria:
Candidate cutoff values are selected by evaluating the shape of peaks on the
histograms; bad cutoff values are rejected by verifying in the image the
compactness of the spatial distribution of the pixels belonging to the peak
determined by the pair of cutoff values. A detailed description of this process
will be given in chapter 3.

2.2.2. Computation of color features using the K-L transformation

At step (2) in figure 2-1, it is important to know what color features are
to be examined. One could use features such as R, G, and B throughout the
segmentation process. However, the color feature which has the deepest valley on
its histogram and that which has the largest discriminant power to separate the
clusters in a given region need not be the same. In the pattern recognition
theory for feature selection, a feature is said to have large discriminant power
if its variance is large. Thus a trial to derive color features with large
discriminant power was made by using the Karhunen-Loeve (K-L) transformation.

More specifically, let S be the region to be segmented, and let Λ be the
covariance matrix of the distributions of R, G, and B in S. Let λ_1, λ_2, and λ_3
be the eigenvalues of Λ, and $\lambda_1 \geq \lambda_2 \geq \lambda_3$. Let $W_i = (w_{Ri} \ w_{Gi} \ w_{Bi})^t$ for i=1, 2, and 3 be
the eigenvectors of Λ corresponding to λ_i, respectively. The color features X_1,
X_2, and X_3 are defined as

$$X_i = w_{Ri}R + w_{Gi}G + w_{Bi}B \qquad (\| W_i \| = 1, \ i=1,2 \text{ and } 3). \qquad (2-1)$$

It is well known that X_1, X_2, and X_3 are uncorrelated, and X_1 is the "best"
feature in the sense that it has the largest variance (the value is λ_1). X_2 is
the best one among the features orthogonal to X_1. At each step of segmenting a
region, three new color features X_1, X_2, and X_3 are calculated for the pixels in
that region and used to compute the histograms. We call this scheme
"segmentation by the dynamic K-L transformation".

The eight scenes shown in figure 2-2 were used in the experiments. The
names of the scenes are (a) cylinder, (b) building, (c) seaside, (d) girl, (e)
room, (f) home, (g) auto, and (h) face. They were digitized with 256×256 spatial

14

resolution and 6-bit density resolution for each of R, G, and B. Scenes (a), (b), and (c) in figure 2-2 were digitized at Kyoto University. (d) is from the University of Southern California, and (e) through (h) are from Carnegie-Mellon University. Scene (a) is a cylinder with color stripes illuminated from the front. Scenes (e), (g), and (h) are the images which Ohlander used in his experiment [Ohlander, 1975], except that the size and density resolution are reduced for our system. Scene (f) is almost the same as Ohlander's "home" scene except that there are some clouds in the sky.

Figure 2-3 shows the results of segmentation by the dynamic K-L transformation. One will notice that use of the "best" color features calculated adaptively at each step of segmenting a region gives satisfying results. In the cylinder scene, for example, the horizontal color stripes are separated almost completely, and the vertical cracks which split the color stripes vertically because of differences in intensity are relatively few. However, using the K-L transformation on the fly requires costly computation and is not very practical. Our goal is to discover a set of color features with which one can achieve segmentations as good as those based on the dynamic K-L transformation.

2.2.3. A set of effective color features

Table 2-1 shows the eigenvectors of Λ for the whole image of each of the eight color scenes in figure 2-2. It is interesting to note that W_1 is approximately $(1/3 \ 1/3 \ 1/3)^t$ for every scene. W_2 is dominated by $(1/2 \ 0 \ -1/2)^t$ or $(-1/2 \ 0 \ 1/2)^t$, and W_3 by $(-1/4 \ 1/2 \ -1/4)^t$. Then it is possible to say that the three orthogonal color features, $I_1=(R+G+B)/3$, $I_2=(R-B)/2$ or $(B-R)/2$, and $I_3=(2G-R-B)/4$, are important components for representing color information.

To prove this experimentally, the linear combinations of R, G, and B, which are used to find the cutoff values for thresholding in segmentation by the dynamic K-L transformation for the eight scenes, are analyzed. Only those cases are examined in which regions with an area larger than 1000 are split into regions larger than 200. The number of linear combinations thus gathered is 109 in this experiment. Those weight vectors are plotted on a w_R-w_B plane as shown in figure 2-4. The weight vectors have been normalized so that $w_G \geq 0$ and $|w_R|+|w_G|+|w_B|=1$. For simplicity, each vector is plotted with the first letter of the name of the scene for which that color feature was used. The weight vectors corresponding to $\{I_1, I_2, I_3\}$, $\{Y, I, Q\}$, $\{X, Y, Z\}$, $\{U, V, W\}$, and $\{R, G, B\}$ are indicated for reference. Contour lines are drawn to show equidistance from the reference points $I_1=(R+G+B)/3$, $I_2=(R-B)/2$ or $(B-R)/2$, and

15

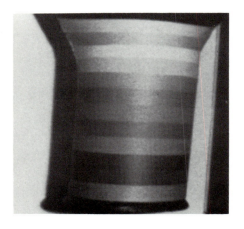

(a) cylinder

(b) building

(c) seaside

(d) girl

Figure 2-2. Color scenes used in the experiments.

(e) room

(f) home

(g) auto

(h) face

Figure 2-2. (continued.)

(a) cylinder

(b) building

(c) seaside

(d) girl

Figure 2-3.   Segmentation results by the dynamic
K-L transformation.

18

(e) room   (f) home

(g) auto   (h) face

Figure 2-3.   (continued.)

Table 2-1. Eigenvectors of Λ for a whole image.

	w_{R1}	w_{G1}	w_{B1}	w_{R2}	w_{G2}	w_{B2}	w_{R3}	w_{G3}	w_{B3}
cylinder	0.269	0.363	0.367	0.469	0.095	-0.437	-0.308	0.461	-0.231
building	0.269	0.340	0.391	0.479	0.103	-0.418	-0.296	0.485	-0.219
seaside	0.258	0.380	0.362	-0.585	0.056	0.358	-0.176	0.464	-0.360
girl	0.336	0.354	0.309	-0.493	0.193	0.314	-0.094	0.474	-0.436
room	0.193	0.341	0.467	0.612	0.079	-0.310	-0.209	0.507	-0.284
home	0.197	0.328	0.476	0.492	0.180	-0.328	-0.313	0.484	-0.204
auto	0.304	0.317	0.378	0.239	0.309	-0.452	-0.514	0.450	0.036
face	0.175	0.411	0.414	0.523	0.128	-0.349	-0.295	0.416	-0.289

normalized by $w_G > 0$, $|w_R| + |w_G| + |w_B| = 1$.

$I_3 = (2G-R-B)/4$. The curves are defined by

$$(w_R-1/3)^2 + (w_G-1/3)^2 + (w_B-1/3)^2 = \epsilon \quad \text{(around } I_1 \text{)},$$
$$(w_R-1/2)^2 + w_G^2 + (w_B+1/2)^2 = \epsilon \quad \text{(around } I_2 \text{)},$$
$$(w_R+1/2)^2 + w_G^2 + (w_B-1/2)^2 = \epsilon \quad \text{(around } I_2 \text{)},$$
$$(w_R+1/4)^2 + (w_G-1/2)^2 + (w_B+1/4)^2 = \epsilon \quad \text{(around } I_3 \text{)},$$
$$(\epsilon = 1/81, \ 1/27, \ 1/9, \ 1/6). \qquad (2-2)$$

Color features in the first quadrant have weight vectors such that $w_R, w_G, w_B \geq 0$. They correspond mainly to the intensity component and $I_1 = (R+G+B)/3$ is the most typical feature of this quadrant. In the second and fourth quadrants, w_R and w_B have opposite signs, and the color features in these quadrants represent the difference of the R and B components. Most color features are in the first quadrant. This means that the intensity is the most important feature even in color image processing.

The weight vector of I_1 is nearly at the center of the weight vectors in the first quadrant as shown in figure 2-4. I_2 can be regarded as being at the center of the weight vectors in the second and fourth quadrants. I_3 will be a

20

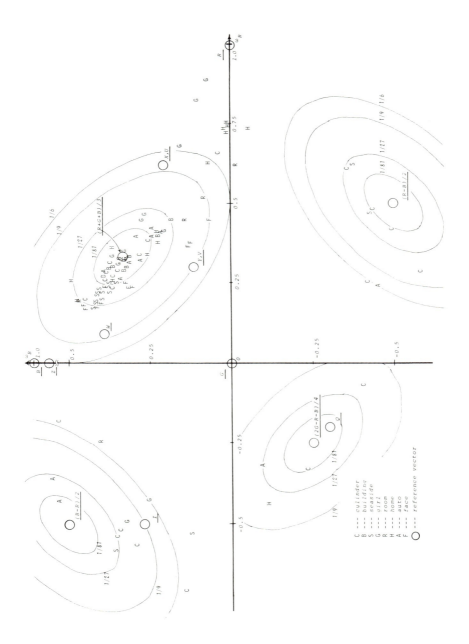

Figure 2-4.   Plots of the weight vectors of 109 color features used in segmentation by the dynamic K-L transformation.

21

typical color feature in the third quadrant. Thus, it is possible to assume that every weight vector in the four quadrants can be approximated by the weight vectors of the three color features, I_1, I_2, and I_3. The numbers of weight vectors in the first, second/fourth, and third quadrants in figure 2-4 are 83, 22, and 4, respectively. So, I_1, I_2, and I_3 are assumed to be significant in this order.

2.2.4. Segmentation by the new color features

We have performed the following experiments to verify the arguments described above.

(1) Segmentation by using three color features I_1, I_2', and I_3'

Figure 2-5 shows the results obtained by using the set of three fixed color features I_1, $I_2'=(R-B)$, and $I_3'=(2G-R-B)/2$. They seem not to be degraded compared with those obtained by the dynamic K-L transformation. This verifies the argument that the set of three color features I_1, I_2', and I_3' can approximate all color features which are calculated as the "best" ones at each important step in segmenting the eight color scenes.

(2) Segmentation by using two color features I_1 and I_2'

In figure 2-4 the number of color features in the third quadrant is only four. They are considerably fewer than those in the other quadrants. Thus the omission of I_3' will not significantly affect the quality of the segmentation. This is verified by the results shown in figure 2-6 which are obtained by using only the two color features, I_1 and I_2'. A picture indicating the missing boundaries from figure 2-5 to figure 2-6 is shown in figure 2-7 for the cylinder scene in order to aid visual comparison. Even in the cylinder scene, which has two weight vectors in the third quadrant, the results of figure 2-5-a and figure 2-6-a are almost the same except that the fifth and sixth color stripes, golden yellow and orange, are not separated in figure 2-6-a.

(3) Segmentation by using only one color feature I_1

What quality of segmentation can be achieved by using only one color feature I_1, i.e., intensity information? In the case of the cylinder scene, the fraction of the number of weight vectors in the first quadrant is 10 out of 22 weight vectors, and there are 10 weight vectors in the second and fourth quadrants. Therefore the quality of the segmentation for the cylinder scene will

(a) cylinder

(b) home

(c) room

Figure 2-5. Segmentation results by using I_1, I_2', and I_3'.
$I_1 = (R+G+B)/3$, $I_2' = (R-B)$, $I_3' = (2G-R-B)/2$.

(a) cylinder

(b) home

(c) room

Figure 2-6.   Segmentation results by using I_1 and I_2'.
$I_1 = (R+G+B)/3$, $I_2' = (R-B)$.

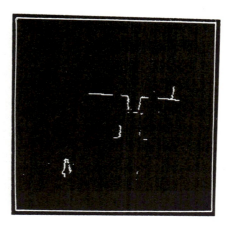

Figure 2-7. Missing boundaries from Fig. 2-5-a to Fig. 2-6-a.

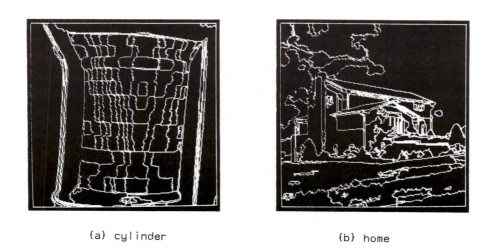

(a) cylinder   (b) home

Figure 2-8. Segmentation results by using only I_1.

(c) room

Figure 2-8.   (continued.)

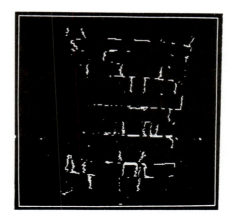

Figure 2-9.   Missing boundaries from Fig. 2-5-a to Fig. 2-8-a.

be considerably degraded by omitting the color feature I_2'. For the other scenes, however, only a few weight vectors are in the second and fourth quadrants and the degradation will not be so significant. The results obtained by using only I_1 are shown in figure 2-8. Figure 2-9 shows the missing boundaries from figure 2-5-a to figure 2-8-a. Separation of the color stripes in the cylinder scene is very poor as expected. This is a natural consequence of losing the distinguishability of color difference by omitting I_2' and I_3'. In the case of the room scene, however, the quality of segmentation is not so much degraded though there appears to be a little missegmentation. As for the home scene in figure 2-8-b, there is no missegmentation, in the sense that the regions which should be segmented are all segmented.

2.3. Comparison of Color Features

2.3.1. Segmentation by various sets of color features

In order to test the effectiveness of the color feature set obtained in the previous section, the eight scenes used in the previous experiments were also segmented using seven sets of color features which are commonly used in image analysis. The sets are {R, G, B}, {X, Y, Z}, {Y, I, Q}, {L, a, b}, {U*, V*, W*}, {I_1, S, H}, and {I_1, r, g}. R, G, and B are the original tristimulus values. X, Y, and Z correspond to the C.I.E. X-Y-Z primary color coordinate system. Y-I-Q is the color coordinate system for television signals. The L-a-b color coordinate system is designed to agree with the Munsell color system. U*-V*-W* is designed to obtain a color solid for which unit shifts in luminance and chrominance are uniformly perceptible [Pratt, 1978]. I_1, S, and H are the intensity, saturation, and hue, respectively. r and g are the normalized colors. Other sets of color features such as {U, V, W}, {S, θ, W*}, and {u, v, V} are not examined because they are similar to the sets {X, Y, Z}, {I_1, S, H}, and {I_1, r, g}, respectively.

{Y, I, Q} and {X, Y, Z} were calculated from {R, G, B} in our experiments by

$$\begin{pmatrix} Y \\ I \\ Q \end{pmatrix} = \begin{pmatrix} 0.299 & 0.587 & 0.114 \\ 0.500 & -0.230 & -0.270 \\ 0.202 & -0.500 & 0.298 \end{pmatrix} \begin{pmatrix} R \\ G \\ B \end{pmatrix},$$

(2-3)

27

$$\begin{pmatrix} X \\ Y \\ Z \end{pmatrix} = \begin{pmatrix} 0.618 & 0.177 & 0.205 \\ 0.299 & 0.587 & 0.114 \\ 0.000 & 0.056 & 0.944 \end{pmatrix} \begin{pmatrix} R \\ G \\ B \end{pmatrix} . \qquad (2\text{-}4)$$

The transformation matrices are not the standard ones; the weights for I, Q, X, and Z are rescaled to normalize the range of the transformed values to be the same as the original R, G, and B. {L, a, b} and {U^*, V^*, W^*} are defined as

$$L = W^* = 25(100Y/Y_0)^{1/3} - 16 ,$$
$$a = 500[(X/X_0)^{1/3} - (Y/Y_0)^{1/3}] ,$$
$$b = 200[(Y/Y_0)^{1/3} - (Z/Z_0)^{1/3}] ,$$
$$U^* = 13W^*(u - u_0) ,$$
$$V^* = 13W^*(v - v_0) , \qquad (2\text{-}5)$$

where $u_0=0.199$, $v_0=0.308$, $u=4X/(X+15Y+3Z)$, $v=6Y/(X+15Y+3Z)$, and X_0, Y_0, Z_0 are the X-Y-Z values for the reference white. Normalized colors, intensity, saturation, and hue are obtained as follows:

$$r = R/(R+G+B), \quad g = G/(R+G+B), \quad b = B/(R+G+B),$$
$$I_1 = (R+G+B)/3,$$
$$S = 1 - 3(\min(r, g, b)),$$
$$H = \arctan2(3^{1/2}(G-B), (2R-G-B)). \qquad (2\text{-}6)$$

There are two problems in using these color features for region segmentation. One is the instability of nonlinear transformations. Normalized color, U^*, V^*, and saturation become unstable and meaningless when R+G+B is small. Therefore, in segmenting a region they are not used to compute histograms if R+G+B is less than 30. Hue is unstable when saturation is near zero, and is not used if S×(R+G+B) is less than 9. The other problem is caused by the fact that the input R, G, and B data are digitized. The histograms of the transformed values from digital input may have a comb-like structure. In order to avoid this, the input R, G, and B values are "undigitized" by adding a random number uniformly selected from the unit interval [Kender,1976].

Figures 2-10 through 2-16 show the results of segmentation obtained by using the seven sets of color features. Comparison of these results will be given in the following section.

28

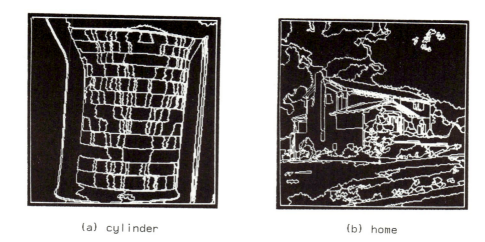

(a) cylinder   (b) home

Figure 2-10.   Segmentation results by using R, G, and B.

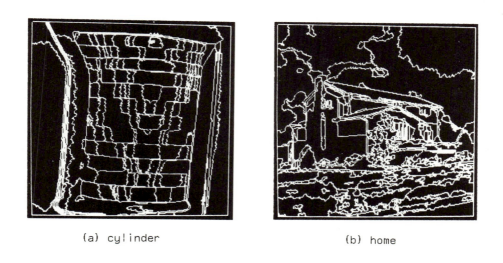

(a) cylinder   (b) home

Figure 2-11.   Segmentation results by using X, Y, and Z.

29

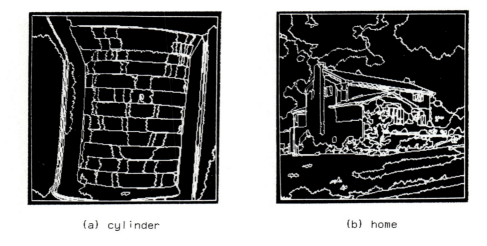

(a) cylinder   (b) home

Figure 2-12.   Segmentation results by using Y, I, and Q.

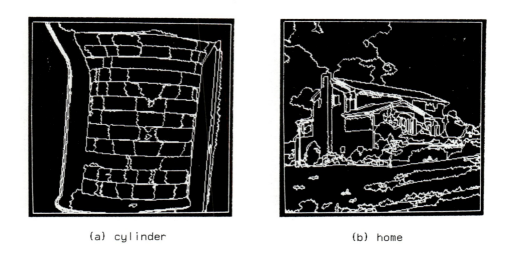

(a) cylinder   (b) home

Figure 2-13.   Segmentation results by using L, a, and b.

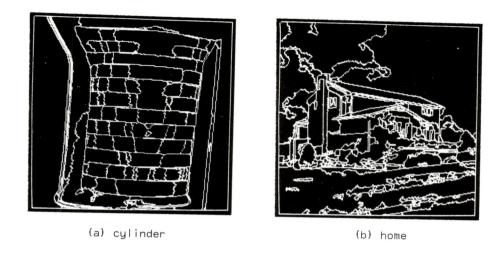

(a) cylinder   (b) home

Figure 2-14. Segmentation results by using U^*, V^*, and W^*.

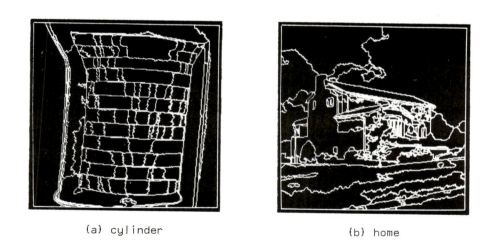

(a) cylinder   (b) home

Figure 2-15. Segmentation results by using I_1, r, and g.

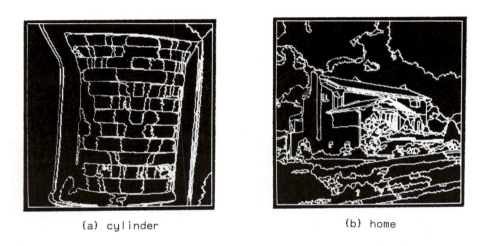

(a) cylinder   (b) home

Figure 2-16. Segmentation results by using I_1, S, and H.

2.3.2. Comparison of color features

The effectiveness of a set of color features used in the segmentation process can be evaluated in terms of the quality of segmentation results and the behavior of the transformation from the input tristimulus values R, G, and B.

Evaluation of the quality of segmentation results is very difficult. No quantative evaluation procedure has been established for the segmentation of natural scenes. Human eyes may be the most reliable tool at present. Pictures which indicate the difference between a pair of segmentation results are generated to help visual comparison as shown in figures 2-7 and 2-9. We think that under-segmentation (failure to split the regions that must be separated) affects later processing more seriously than does over-segmentation (splitting the regions that need not be separated). So the evaluation criteria are set more severely against under-segmentation than over-segmentation.

{R, G, B}

Use of the color feature set {R, G, B} for segmentation requires no transformation. But R, G and B have a strong factor of intensity and are heavily correlated. Thus, spurious segmentation tends to occur because of differences in intensity. This tendency is clearly observed in figure 2-10-a. Note that the vertical splitting of color stripes occurs more frequently in figure 2-10-a than in figure 2-5-a which is segmented by using the set of I_1, I_2', and I_3'.

{X, Y, Z}

The weight vectors of X, Y, and Z are located in the first quadrant of the w_R-w_B plane as shown in figure 2-4; i.e., all have a strong factor of intensity. This implies that the use of this set will result in a segmentation similar to that obtained by using R, G, and B (see figures 2-10-a and 2-11-a). The separation of the color stripes in figure 2-11-a is worse than figure 2-10-a, because the weight vectors of X and Y are closer to the white point (I_1) in figure 2-4 than those of R and G.

{Y, I, Q}

Y, I, and Q are in the first, second, and third quadrants, respectively (see figure 2-4). The segmentation results obtained by using {Y, I, Q} (figure 2-12) are similar to those obtained by using {I_1, I_2', I_3'} (figure 2-5). In figure 2-12-a the uppermost two color stripes are not separated, while they are separated in figure 2-5-a. The reason is that the weight vector of color

33

feature I, located at a biased position in the fourth quadrant, is not a good approximation of the color features in the second quadrant. A more important difference between $\{Y, I, Q\}$ and $\{I_1, I_2', I_3'\}$ is in the calculation of these features from $\{R, G, B\}$. The computation of $\{Y, I, Q\}$ from $\{R, G, B\}$ requires floating-point multiplications. Furthermore, there is the possibility that spurious combs appear in the histograms of Y, I, and Q. In contrast, all coefficients of the transformation from $\{R, G, B\}$ to $\{I_1, I_2', I_3'\}$ are of the form $1/i$, where i is an integer. This means that a comb-like structure never appears in the histograms of I_1, I_2', I_3'. The calculation of $\{I_1, I_2', I_3'\}$ from $\{R, G, B\}$ is far simpler than that of $\{Y, I, Q\}$. It can be performed by addition and subtraction of integer numbers together with shifting or simple table-lookup operations for scaling.

$\{L, a, b\}$ and $\{U^*, V^*, W^*\}$

Figure 2-13 shows the result obtained by using the set $\{L, a, b\}$, and figure 2-14 is the result obtained by using the set $\{U^*, V^*, W^*\}$. Both color coordinate systems use cube-root features for luminance as shown in equation 2-5. This results in the good performance in separation of the color stripes at the left side of the cylinder where intensity is dark and gradually changes. L, a, and b are based on the Y, (X-Y), and (Y-Z) color features which are located in tne first, third, and fourth quadrant, respectively. On the other hand, U^*, V^*, and W^* are based on the u-v-V normalized color coordinate system which is derived from the U-V-W system, and U, V, and W are all located in the first quadrant in figure 2-4. This causes the missegmentation at the border of pale-yellow and yellow stripes and the missegmentation at the border of golden-yellow and orange stripes in the strongly illuminated part of the cylinder surface in figure 2-14-a, while in figure 2-13-a all color stripes are separated clearly. In the case of the home scene (and in the other scenes), the figures do not show significant differences among the segmentation results obtained by these two sets of features and the other sets of features.

$\{I_1, r, g\}$ and $\{I_1, S, H\}$

The set of color features $\{I_1, r, g\}$ produces the result shown in figure 2-15. The use of color features normalized by intensity results in good segmentation in the dark part of the cylinder scene; it is as good as the results obtained by using $\{L, a, b\}$ or $\{U^*, V^*, W^*\}$. Highly illuminated parts of the border between the pale-yellow and yellow stripes are not separated as in

34

Table 2-2.　Variances of I_1, I_2, and I_3 images.

	σ_{I1}^{2}	σ_{I2}^{2}	σ_{I3}^{2}
cylinder	92.4	6.5	1.1
building	97.0	2.8	0.1
seaside	80.6	17.0	2.4
girl	85.8	10.4	3.8
room	75.2	22.7	2.2
home	76.7	19.5	3.8
auto	89.9	6.4	3.7
face	87.7	9.6	2.8

scaled by $\sigma_{I1}^{2}+\sigma_{I2}^{2}+\sigma_{I3}^{2}=100$.

the result for {U*, V*, W*}. Figure 2-16 is the result for {I_1, S, H}. It seems to be more degraded than that obtained by using {I_1, r, g} shown in figure 2-15. One reason is that the hue can be meaningful only in limited cases. From the computational point of view, these nonlinear transformations incur far more cost than linear transformations.

Table 2-2 shows the variances, σ_{I1}^{2}, σ_{I2}^{2}, and σ_{I3}^{2}, of the three components of a color image represented in the I_1-I_2-I_3 color space. The variances are scaled so that $\sigma_{I1}^{2}+\sigma_{I2}^{2}+\sigma_{I3}^{2}=100$ for each color image.

Note that $\sigma_{I1}^{2}>\sigma_{I2}^{2}>\sigma_{I3}^{2}$ for every color image. This relation corresponds to tne fact that (the number of color features in the first quadrant) > (the number of color features in the second/fourth quadrant) > (the number of color features in the third quadrant) in figure 2-4. Thus, it can be said that color features with larger variance are more useful in region segmentation of a color image.

Our experiments also say that chromatic information is not always important for the segmentation process even in case of colorful scenes which have large variance in the chromatic components. We think that the usefulness of a color feature is greatly influenced by the structure of the color scenes to be

Table 2-3. Eigenvalues of Λ for a whole image.

	$\lambda 1$	$\lambda 2$	$\lambda 3$
cylinder	94.0	5.3	0.7
building	99.2	0.7	0.1
seaside	82.3	16.7	1.0
girl	86.0	11.7	2.3
room	81.8	16.1	2.1
home	84.2	12.1	3.6
auto	90.7	7.7	1.7
face	97.4	2.2	0.4

scaled by $\lambda 1 + \lambda 2 + \lambda 3 = 100$.

segmented. For instance, the variance of I_2 is only 6.5 in the cylinder scene where I_2 plays an important role in segmentation, while the variance of I_2 is 19.5 in the home scene which was segmented well by using I_1 alone. This phenomenon can be explained by the difference in the structures of the cylinder and home scenes. The cylinder scene consists of a curved surface, while the home scene includes mainly planar objects. The intensity gradually changes on the curved surfaces, and it does not work as a useful feature for segmenting the color stripes. This may be the reason why chromatic features were frequently used in the segmentation of the cylinder scene.

2.4. Two Component Representation of Color Images

Table 2-3 shows the eigenvalues, λ_1, λ_2, and λ_3, of the covariance matrix Λ obtained for the R, G, and B data in tne whole image of each color scene. The values nave been scaled such that $\lambda_1+\lambda_2+\lambda_3=100$. λ_3 is very small for every scene; the maximum value is 3.6. This implies that each color image can be approximated by two features X_1 and X_2 with a mean-square error of 3.6 at maximum: X_1 and X_2 are the linear combinations of R, G, and B with weights λ_1

36

and λ_2, respectively. We tried to compose color images from only two features X_1 and X_2 by using the incomplete inverse of the K-L transformation.

Let W be the 3×3 matrix for the K-L transformation of a color image.

$$(X_1\ X_2\ X_3\ )^t = W\ (R\ G\ B)^t\ . \tag{2-7}$$

Of course this transformation is reversible and

$$(R\ G\ B)^t = W^{-1}(X_1\ X_2\ X_3\ )^t\ . \tag{2-8}$$

Now suppose X_3 is fixed to be M_3 throughout the image, since the variance of X_3 is small. Here, M_3 is the mean value of X_3 for the whole image. Then one can consider a color image reconstructed by this inverse mapping from the two features X_1, X_2, and constant M_3 for X_3. The color components of each pixel are given by

$$(R'\ G'\ B')^t = W^{-1}(X_1\ X_2\ M_3\ )^t\ . \tag{2-9}$$

We compared the color images defined by R', G', and B' with the original color images. Figures 2-17 through 2-20 show the results of the experiments. In each figure, (a) is the reconstructed color image and (b) is the original color image. Images (c), (d), and (e) represent X_1, X_2, and X_3, respectively. The following two facts were observed: (1) Although the R'-G'-B' color images are composed by using only two spectral features, they are good reconstructions of the original color images. (2) The clarity of color in a small area in the color image tends to be heavily degraded. The first fact means that the color information in the scenes used in the experiments is almost two dimensional. The second fact can be explained by examining the images corresponding to X_3. The remarkable low contrast is due to its small variance. However, there exist noticable small areas with a different gray value from the average. These areas have vivid colors, and they can not be fully represented by the two principal features X_1 and X_2. Thus, their colors are spoiled by neglecting X_3. To sum up, color images can be represented by using only two spectral features at the cost of spoiling the clarity of the colors of small areas. The experiments by Land [Land, 1959] tell us that the colors in natural images are "perceptually" almost two dimensional; our eyes can perceive full colors by mixing two spectral

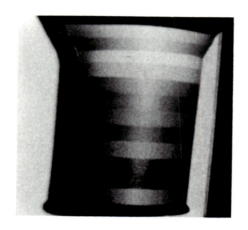

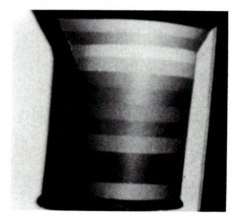

(a) reconstructed image   (b) original image

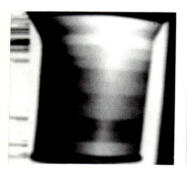

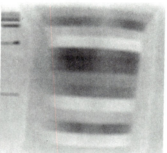

(c) image of X_1 (d) image of X_2 (e) image of X_3

Figure 2-17.   Reconstruction of color images by using X_1 and X_2: Example 1. Cylinder. (See color section opposite page 72 for color reproduction of (a) and (b).)

(a) reconstructed image   (b) original image

  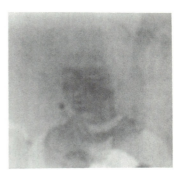

(c) image of X_1 (d) image of X_2 (e) image of X_3

Figure 2-18.   Reconstruction of color images by using X_1 and X_2:
Example 2. Girl. (See color section opposite page 72 for color
reproduction of (a) and (b).)

39

(a) reconstructed image   (b) original image

(c) image of X_1 (d) image of X_2 (e) image of X_3

Figure 2-19.   Reconstruction of color images by using X_1 and X_2:
Example 3. Room. (See color section opposite page 72 for color
reproduction of (a) and (b).)

40

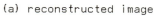

(a) reconstructed image   (b) original image

(c) image of X_1 (d) image of X_2 (e) image of X_3

Figure 2-20.   Reconstruction of color images by using X_1 and X_2:
Example 4. Home. (See color section opposite page 72 for color
reproduction of (a) and (b).)

41

stimuli in the context of natural images. The experiment described here shows that the color in natural scenes is "physically" almost two dimensional.

2.5. Conclusion

We have considered the role of color information in the region segmentation process. By means of systematic experiments in region segmentation, we found a set of effective color features $I_1 = (R+G+B)/3$, $I_2' = (R-B)$, and $I_3' = (2G-R-B)/2$. The three features are significant in this order and in many cases good segmentations can be achieved by using only the first two. The transformation to derive them from the R, G, and B data is simple and it does not behave badly even when digitized input is used.

Comparisons were made experimentally between various sets of color features which are commonly used in image analysis. The characteristics of each set can be observed through the comparative experiments. The differences among segmentation results appear clearly in the case of the cylinder scene in which the separation of the color stripes is difficult. The color feature sets {L, a, b} and {I_1, I_2', I_3'} give good results in our experiments. But in many other scenes, no significant difference is observed among the results obtained by using the eight sets of color features. This seems to be closely related to the fact that the color information in natural scenes is almost two dimensional (intensity and one chromatic feature), which was shown in the experiment of color image reconstruction by using only two color features. That is, every set of color features can represent the color information for many scenes with a fairly large margin and therefore can provide enough information for region segmentation. When different sets of color features make little difference in the segmentation of a scene, the calculation involved in the coordinate transformation from the R-G-B system becomes an important factor in judging the effectiveness of the color coordinate system for region segmentation. The set of color features derived in this chapter is computationally efficient as well as effective in segmentation. We think that it is a useful color feature set for color image segmentation.

In this chapter, the effectiveness of color features was discussed in the framework of region splitting. The results will be useful in other domains of color image processing such as edge extraction.

3 Preliminary Segmentation of Color Images

3.1. The Problems

3.1.1. Nonpurposive segmentation

Two topics will be described in this chapter. One is the segmentation of a color image into a set of regions based on spectral information. The other is the organization of the segmentation result into a symbolic data structure.

Generally speaking, two processes are necessary for analyzing image patterns: (1) low-level processes which segment the input image and extract useful features from this segmented image; and (2) higher-level processes which perform semantic analysis of the image patterns based on the features extracted in the low-level process. In order to achieve good performance in the segmentation, it has been recognized that it is useful to import task-specific knowledge into the low-level processing. For this, we consider the following four schemes.

Basic scheme   Figure 3-1-a illustrates the basic scheme. First, segmentation and feature extraction are performed on an input image. Second, the extracted features are matched with models which describe the knowledge about the patterns to be analyzed. The task-specific knowledge is used only in the higher-level matching process. When the patterns to be analyzed are complex, it is difficult to obtain a "correct" segmentation, and the feature extraction becomes unreliable.

Top-down scheme   The task-specific knowledge is imported into the low-level process as well as the higher-level process as shown in figure 3-1-b. The segmentation process can be tuned to the patterns to be analyzed. This scheme works well when variation of input patterns is limited, but some defects are inevitable. First, the segmentation algorithms in this scheme are special purpose ones and they often turn out to be powerless when applied to a task slightly different from the one for which the algorithms were originally

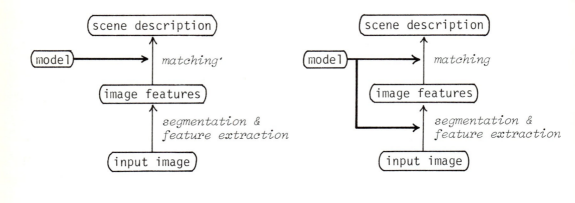

(a) basic scheme   (b) top-down scheme

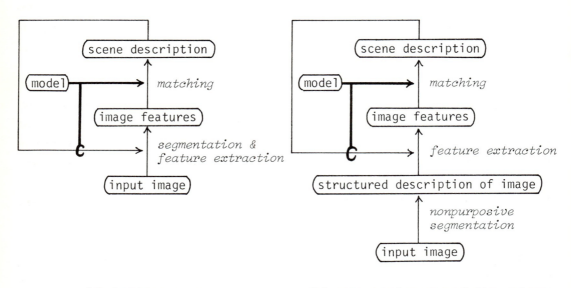

(c) feedback scheme   (d) nonpurposive segmentation scheme

Figure 3-1. Four schemes for importing knowledge into image analysis.

44

designed. Second, it is difficult to apply this scheme to tasks in which sufficient a priori knowledge about input patterns is not available.

Feedback scheme   When the input patterns are very complicated or noisy, a simple top-down scheme cannot cope with them since it is difficult to extract the features necessary for the analysis all at once. The feedback scheme shown in figure 3-1-c has been developed to overcome this difficulty. The results of partial analysis are fed back to the low-level process to guide it in searching for more detailed features. This scheme works effectively when important features which determine the overall structure of input patterns can be extracted rather easily at the initial stage of analysis. Otherwise, the costly operations which deal with the raw image data are apt to be iterated wastefully due to the trial-and-error interplay between the higher and lower level processes.

Nonpurposive segmentation scheme   The feedback scheme tries to extract the features directly from a flood of data, the raw image, by top-down control. If the feature extraction can be performed on a well-organized database, the inefficiency of the feedback scheme will be fairly improved. One way to construct such a database is to segment the input image into a set of edges or regions and to organize them into a structured description. This description represents rich symbolic information that is extracted from the raw image data. Figure 3-1-d illustrates this idea. The merits of making such descriptions are:

1) It is convenient to manipulate the descriptions by high-level languages such as Lisp or FORTRAN. This helps in implementing the higher-level process.
2) The picture processing functions can be executed at high speed without dealing with the raw image.

Once one takes this view, the main role of segmentation is not necessarily to "reduce" the amount of data but to "structure" the data into usable information. Furthermore, the algorithm must be a "nonpurposive" one; it must be applied to a wide range of tasks. Marr's "Primal Sketch" [Marr, 1975] is one way of making such a "nonpurposive" symbolic description of image data. He extracted edge segments in the image by means of various kinds of local filtering and organized them into a set of symbols.

45

We have developed an image analysis system based on this scheme. Regions are employed to describe the image data. The description is called the "Patchery Data Structure".

3.1.2. Specifications for segmentation and symbolic description

An image of the scene is given as red, green, and blue intensity arrays. The "nonpurposive" symbolic description of the image is constructed by two processes: the segmentation process and the description process. The segmentation process extracts the structural information of the image by partitioning it into coherent regions using spectral information. The description of the segmented image must then be organized to facilitate flexible retrieval of pictorial information.

We have settled on the following specifications for the segmentation process.
(a) It deals with color images of 256×256 pixels.
(b) It must extract the detailed structures as well as the global structures in the image .
(c) It should apply to a wide range of tasks; i.e., it must be "nonpurposive".
(d) Segmentations based on texture differences are not considered.
(e) The textural areas should be kept from being broken into too many tiny fragments.
(f) The partition must be performed such that one can assume a single region does not span more than one object in the scene. That is, the partition may go to the state of "over-segmentation".

As for the description, the following specifications are assumed.
(g) The description is to be constructed using regions, boundaries, vertices, etc. as the descriptive elements. The relationships between the regions must be described.
(h) High-speed derivation of the pictorial information from the description must be possible.
(i) The storage size necessary for the description should be small.
(j) The features explicitly included in the description should be limited to the basic ones. Other features are derived from the described ones when they become necessary.

46

3.2. Region Splitting Using Multihistograms

3.2.1. The algorithm

We adopted an algorithm which uses multihistograms of one dimension to find the features to be used for region splitting. The basic idea of the algorithm is as follows: The whole image is first partitioned into sub-images each of which is a connected region; then each sub-image is further partitioned if possible; and this process iterates. This algorithm has been applied by Tomita et al. [1973] to the segmentation of artificial textural patterns. Ohlander [1975] applied it to the segmentation of color scenes.

Because the algorithm uses histograms to find the cues for segmentation, it is suitable for the extraction of global structures in input images. On the other hand, it is weak in detecting the detailed structures. Some improvements are needed to realize a segmentation process which satisfies the specifications described in the previous section.

Figure 3-2 shows a schematic diagram of the segmentation algorithm using multihistograms. Because of the recursive nature of the algorithm, a picture stack is used to store the region masks. A region mask represents a connected

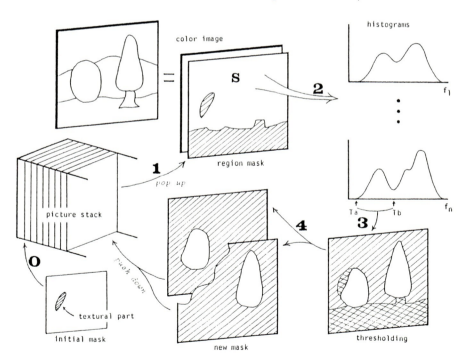

Figure 3-2. Region splitting using multihistograms.

region (the area without hatching in figure 3-2) which is to be examined for segmentation. The segmentation is performed as follows:

1. The textural areas are first extracted (see section 3-2-2). A mask corresponding to the non-textural area is placed at the bottom of the stack. --- The arrow 0 in figure 3-2.
2. If the stack is empty, the algorithm stops. (Segmentation is finished.)
3. One mask is taken from the top of the stack. Let S denote the region represented by the mask (the area without hatching). --- The arrow 1 in figure 3-2.
4. If the region S is small (i.e., the number of the pixels in S is less than a threshold T_1), it is not partitioned further and is memorized as a resultant region; GO TO 2.
5. Histograms of color features in the region S are computed. --- The arrow 2 in figure 3-2.
6. If all histograms are monomodal, the algorithm skips to step (9).
7. If any of the histograms show conspicuous peaks, a pair of cutoff values which separate the peak in the histogram are determined at the position of valleys, and the image of the color feature corresponding to that histogram is thresholded using the cut-off values; thus the region S is partitioned. --- The arrow 3 in figure 3-2.
8. Connected regions (with area greater than a threshold T_2) are extracted. For each connected region, a region mask is generated, and it is pushed down on the stack. --- The arrow 4 in figure 3-2.
    GO TO 2.
9. If the area of the region S is not large (less than a threshold T_3), the region S is memorized as a resultant region, and GO TO 2.
10. Extraction of detailed structures in the region S is tried by the window scanning method (see section 3-2-5). If it succeeds, the region S is partitioned, GO TO 8. Otherwise, the region S is memorized as a resultant region.
    GO TO 2.

    The threshold T_1 is determined to avoid exhaustive trials for splitting small regions. The threshold T_2 is used to reject noisy regions and to prevent meaningless fragmentation. The threshold T_3 is determined in connection with the size of the small windows. In the case of segmenting color images with 256×256

48

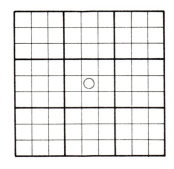

(a) Laplacian operator   (b) 9 × 9 window operator

Figure 3-3.   The Laplacian operator and a 9 × 9 window operator.

pixels,   the thresholds T_1, T_2, and T_3 are set to 50, 8, and 1536,   respectively. Admitting slight over-segmentation,   the quality of the segmentation results is not significantly influenced by changing the threshold values.

3.2.2. Pre-extraction of textural parts

The textural parts (busy parts) in input images are apt to be divided into a lot of meaningless fragments. In order to prevent this, the textural parts are first extracted from the image and the segmentation process is applied only to the parts without texture. The extraction of the textural parts is performed by the following steps.

(1) The Laplacian operator (figure 3-3-a) is applied to the green image to produce a Laplacian image. Thresholding is executed at a cutoff value T to yield an edge image. The green image is used because it is the most similar to the black-and-white image among the three component images. The cutoff value T is determined from the mode value and the standard deviation of the histogram for the Laplacian image.

$$T = (mode\ value) + (standard\ deviation) \times 1.4 \qquad (3-1)$$

(2) Utilizing the 9×9 window shown in figure 3-3-b on the binary picture, if more than 8 of 9 subwindows (3×3) have at least one "1", the central pixel is considered to be textural. The textural pixels which form connected regions with large area are determined to be textural parts.

This method detects the areas with scattered edge segments. It is not sensitive to the sharp edges at boundaries between objects. Figure 3-4 shows the sequence of extraction of textural parts. Figure 3-4-a is an input image, figure 3-4-b is the edge image, and figure 3-4-c shows the textural parts extracted.

3.2.3. Selection of cutoff values using histograms

A pair of cutoff values used to partition the image at step (7) of the segmentation algorithm are selected from the positions of valleys in the histograms.

After a smoothing operation by a kind of local avaraging, all peaks and valleys in the histograms are detected and a score is calculated for each peak (see figure 3-5).

$$\text{score} = ((2P-V_a-V_b)/2P) \times ((W-N_p/P)/W) , \qquad (3-2)$$

where N_p is the number of pixels contained in the peak.

The first term represents the relative depth of the valleys and the second the sharpness of the peak. The deeper valleys and the sharper peak are more desirable. The best three peaks are selected through all the histograms and the positions of their valleys are used as the candidate cutoff values.

3.2.4. Verification of cutoff values by spatial evaluation

A pair of cutoff values with a high score does not necessarily produce a partition with good quality; an accidental partition may occur. It is necessary to test the quality of the partitions that will be obtained by using the candidate cutoff values selected in the histograms and to reject bad partitions.

We define the "looseness" of a binary mask which represents the regions extracted by the thresholding, as follows:

50

(a) input image

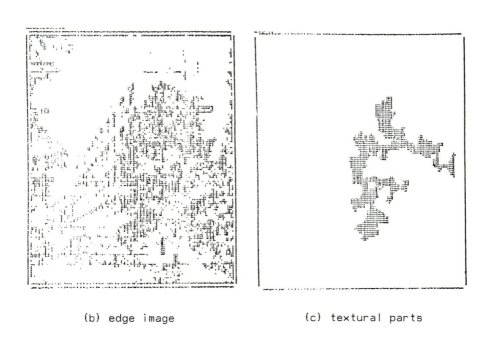

(b) edge image   (c) textural parts

Figure 3-4. An example of textural parts extraction.

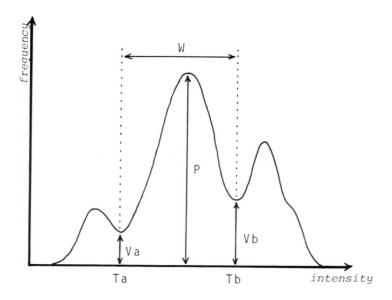

Figure 3-5.   Score for a peak in a histogram.

$$\text{looseness} = ((NF-NO)/NO)^2 + ((NO-NS)/NO)^2 \, , \qquad\qquad (3\text{-}3)$$

    where NO is the number of 1s in the binary picture,
                  NF is the number of 1s after "fusion" operation,
                  NS is the number of 1s after "shrinking" operation.

Roughly speaking, the looseness is related to the ratio of the number of boundary points at which 1s neighbor with 0s, to the total number of 1s; but it can be calculated more quickly than the strict ratio. The way to calculate the looseness is illustrated in figure 3-6. For each partition, the looseness is calculated for both binary pictures. The partition which has the smallest sum of the looseness values is selected as the best.

3.2.5. Detection and extraction of detailed structures

    The segmentation algorithm uses histograms to detect the structures in a region to be examined. In the case of large regions, sometimes no valleys can be detected in any histogram even when the region contains some structures. This is

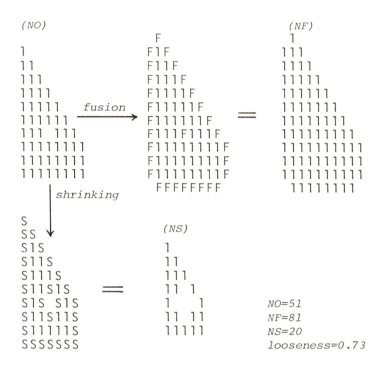

```
(NO)                                    (NF)
                     F                    1
1                    F1F                  111
11                   F11F                 1111
111                  F111F                11111
1111                 F1111F               111111
11111     fusion     F11111F      =       1111111
111111   ────────→   F111111F             11111111
111 111              F111F111F            111111111
11111111             F11111111F           1111111111
11111111             F11111111F           1111111111
11111111             F11111111F           1111111111
                      FFFFFFFF            11111111
      │ shrinking
S     │
SS    ↓
S1S                  (NS)
S11S
S111S                   1
S11S1S      =          11
S1S S1S                111
S11S11S                11 1
S11111S                1   1          NO=51
SSSSSSS                11 11          NF=81
                       11111          NS=20
                                      looseness=0.73
```

Figure 3-6.   Calculation of "looseness" for a binary mask.
              NO is the number of 1s in the mask,
              NF is the number of 1s after "fusion" operation,
              NS is the number of 1s after "shrinking" operation.

because small valleys in a histogram are veiled by dominant peaks or because many small peaks overlap with each other. To cope with such cases, regions with area greater than a threshold are scanned using a window, and the histograms for each window are examined. This operation is illustrated in figure 3-7. The window size is set to 32×32 when the image size is 256×256.

This method works well in detecting the detailed structures in large regions, but the partition should be performed with caution. Strictly speaking,

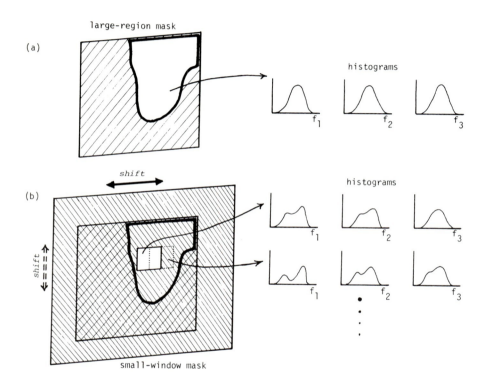

Figure 3-7. Schema of the window-scanning method.
    (a) In large regions sometimes no valley can be detected in any histogram even when the region contains some structures.
    (b) Large regions are scanned by a small window and the histograms for each window are tested.

the cutoff values selected from the histogram for a particular window are valid only for the local area in the window. If the cutoff values are applied to the whole region, undesirable partitions may result as illustrated in figure 3-8. In order to avoid this, after applying the cutoff values to the whole region, only the extracted segments which intersect the window corresponding to the histogram are picked up and partitioned.

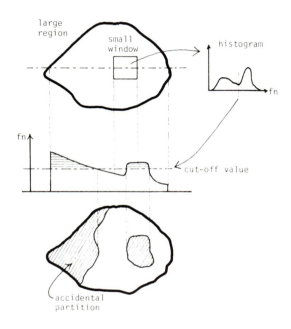

Figure 3-8.   Simple application of a threshold obtained by the
window-scanning method may cause accidental partitions.

The value of the feature fn smoothly changes in the left part of the region, while it changes abruptly in the right part. If the cut-off value selected on the histogram for the window in the right part is applied to the whole region, an accidental partition may happen in the left part.

55

3.3. Representation of the Segmented Image

3.3.1. Patchery Data Structure

The regions obtained as the result of segmentation are recorded as a two dimensional image array. The role of the symbolic description is to arrange the segmentation results into' a well-organized data structure which allows easy derivation of pictorial features related to the properties of and the relations between the regions. The data structure is called the "Patchery Data Structure".

Few results have been reported on a structured description of image data for the purpose of retrieving the pictorial information. Kunii et al. [1974] reported a system which uses a relational model to represent the pictorial information. The primary aim of their system is to build an image database with the ability to retrieve images by specifying their contents. In our case, the primary aim is to retrieve features of an image based on regions. Relationships among regions may be represented by ordered sets with a variable number of elements; for example, a set of boundary segments forms the contour of a region. These relations are conveniently expressed by using pointers. Regions, boundary segments, and vertices are the descriptive elements in the Patchery Data Sturcture, and various kinds of pointers are used to describe relations between the elements.

Figure 3-9 illustrates the definition of regions, boundary segments, and vertices. 4-connectedness is employed to define the regions. The boundary segments are defined on the mesh placed on the interval of the pixels. Each boundary segment corresponds to the border between two regions and it is represented by chain codes (with 4 directions) from the start vertex to the end vertex. Each vertex is a start or end point of a boundary segment between two regions. A vertex is the corner point at which three or four regions meet.

Holes and line segments are also the descriptive elements. A hole is a group of regions which is surrounded by another region. A line segment corresponds to a linear section of a boundary segment. The iterative end-point fits method [Duda and Hart,1973] is used to fit line segments to the chain code of a boundary segment. Figure 3-10 illustrates the line fitting operations. The method is simple, but effective.

3.3.2. Primary features and secondary features

The description must support high-speed derivation of various kinds of features when they become necessary in the analysis process. One possible scheme

56

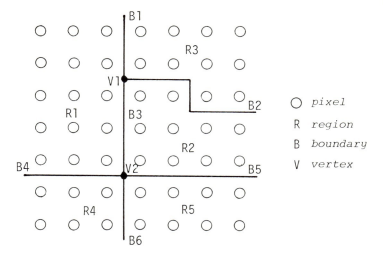

Figure 3-9. Regions, boundary segments, and vertices.

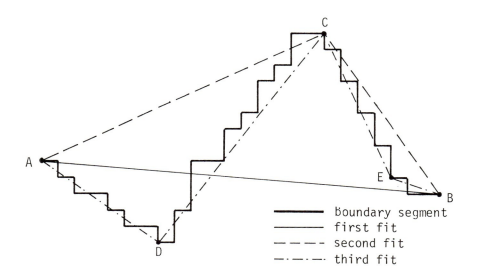

boundary segment
first fit
second fit
third fit

Figure 3-10. The iterative end-point fits method.
A and B are the end-points (vertices) of the boundary segment. The line AB is initially fit to the boundary. The distances from each point on the boundary to this line are computed, and if all the distances are less than a threshold the process is finished. If not, the point C, furthest from the line AB, is found and the line AB is blocken into two new lines AC and CB. This process iterates.

57

needed in the analysis process is calculated beforehand
tion. But this is infeasible for the following two
ul to calculate features which may not be used in the
large amount of storage would be necessary to store all
es.

in the image analysis can be divided into two classes:
and secondary features. The calculation of a primary feature
with the image arrays and generally is time consuming. On the
the secondary features, such as compactness of a region, can be
from a set of primary features, and their calculation can be
quickly. Based on such considerations, only the primary features are
in our description. The secondary features will be calculated from the
y features of the descriptive elements and their relationships when needed
ne analysis process.

3.3.3. Description of properties

The properties of regions, boundary segments, vertices, holes, and line segments are described in each descriptive element. Table 3-1 shows the features used for the description as the properties of descriptive elements. For a region, the following features are described (figure 3-11).

(1) Area --- The number of pixels included in the region.
(2) Mean intensities of R, G, and B data.
(3) Degree of texture --- The mean value of the operator in figure 3-3-b.
(4) Contour length --- The total length of the boundaries which surround the region.
(5) Position of the mass center --- The position vector M=(MX, MY) of mass center of a region is computed as follows:

$$M = (1/N) \sum_{i=1}^{N} P_i \; , \tag{3-4}$$

where N is the number of pixels in the region,
P$_i$ is the position vector of i-th pixel.

(6) Minimum bounding rectangle (MBR) --- The MBR is defined as a set of four figures XMIN, XMAX, YMIN, and YMAX. They are the maximum and minimum values of the X and Y coordinates of the pixel positions in the region.

58

Table 3-1. Primary features for each descriptive element.

descriptive element	primary features
region	area; mean intensities of R, G, and B; degree of texture; contour length; position of the mass center; number of holes; scatter matrix of pixel positions; minimum bounding rectangle (MBR).
boundary segment	chain codes; length; contrast.
vertex	position; number of boundary segments.
hole	contour length.
line segment	distance from origin (ρ); orientation (θ); length; positions of end points.

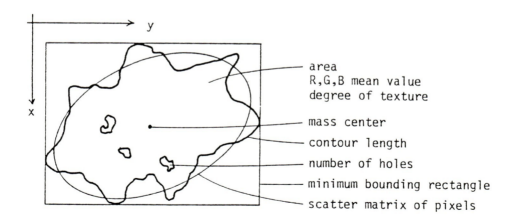

Figure 3-11. Description of a region.

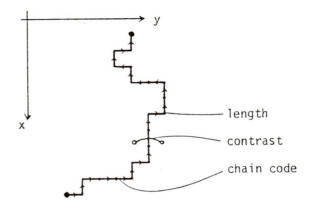

Figure 3-12.   Description of a boundary segment.

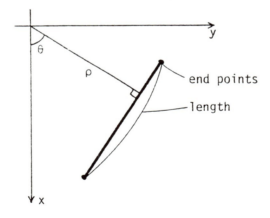

Figure 3-13.   Description of a line segment.

(7) Scatter matrix --- The scatter matrix represents the elliptical area which approximates the shape of the region. It is more useful than the minimum bounding rectangle. The scatter matrix C of a region can be calculated as follows:

$$C = (1/N) \sum_{i=1}^{N} (P_i-M) (P_i-M)^t \quad ,$$ (3-5)

where N is the number of pixels in the region,

P_i denotes the position vector of i-th pixel,

M denotes the mass center of the region.

Figure 3-12 illustrates the features described for boundary segments. The contrast is the mean difference of R, G, and B values across the boundary segment.

Figure 3-13 shows the features for line segments. A polar coordinate system (ρ-θ system) is used to represent a line segment. The ρ-θ system is convenient to aggregate collinear line segments.

3.3.4. Description of relations

Topological relations   The topological relations among regions, boundary segments, vertices, holes and line segments are expressed by the pointers between each descriptive element. Figure 3-14 illustrates the pointers used in the Patchery Data Structure. The meaning of the pointers will be clear from the figure.   The boundary segments which form the contour of a region or a hole are ordered counter-clockwise. According to the considerations in section 3-3-2, only the "primary relations" are explicitly represented. Other relations can be derived from the primary ones when they become necessary.   For example, the set of regions touching a certain region can be obtained as follows: (1) Using the "contour-set" relation, the set of boundary segments surrounding the region is derived; (2) using the "both-sides" relation, regions which share the boundary segments with that region are gathered as the objective set.

Color relations   It is useful to describe the relationships among regions which have similar colors. The basic operation of the segmentation algorithm using multihistograms, which we employed in our system, is to extract regions with a similar spectral property. A segmentation tree which records the history

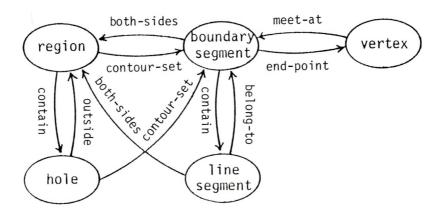

Figure 3-14.   Description of topological relations.

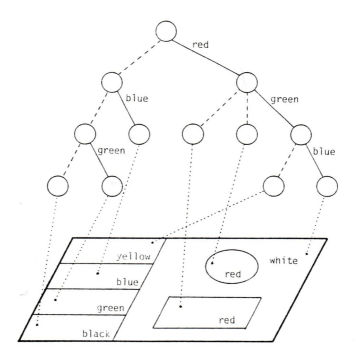

Figure 3-15.   Description of color relations.

of segmentation can be used to describe the color relations among the regions. Figure 3-15 is an example of the segmentation tree. Each node in the tree corresponds to a region. The root-node corresponds to the whole image and the leaf-nodes correspond to the elementary regions obtained as the final result of the segmentaion. Every node except the leaf-node has its child-nodes which correspond to the regions obtained by splitting the region corresponding to that node. There are two kinds of child-node: sons and daughters. The sons correspond to the regions which are extracted by the cutoff operation from the parent region. The daughters correspond to the remaining regions. The cutoff values used to separate the region are recorded in the corresponding node.

The distance between two nodes in the segmentation tree is defined as the path length between them. Regions which are nearby in the segmentation tree have similar colors. But it can not be said that distant nodes have very different colors. Furthermore, the color relation represented by the entire segmentation tree depends on the color features which are used for the segmentation process; i.e., the segmentation tree created by using R, G, and B is different from that created by using Y, I, and Q. In spite of such difficulties, we think that the segmentation tree will be a useful tool for retrieving the regions based on similarity of color.

3.4. Manipulation of the Patchery Data Structure

3.4.1. Merging of regions

In region-oriented image analyses, it is often necessary to merge several regions into one. In such a case, the features in table 3-1 of a new region should be calculated from the features of the old regions without referring back to the image arrays. In our system, this can be performed as follows.

(1) Mean intensities of R, G, and B data, degree of texture, position of mass center --- The feature f of the new region can be calculated by the weighted average.

$$f = (\sum_{i=1}^{N} f_i * S_i)/\sum_{i=1}^{N} S_i , \qquad (3-6)$$

where S_i and f_i denote, respectively, the area and the feature of the i-th old region.

(2) Minimum bounding rectangle (MBR) --- The MBR (XMIN, XMAX, YMIN, YMAX) of the new region can be obtained as the MBR of the MBRs of old regions.

$$XMIN = minimum \{ XMIN_i \} ,$$
$$XMAX = maximum \{ XMAX_i \} ,$$
$$YMIN = minimum \{ YMIN_i \} ,$$
$$YMAX = maximum \{ YMAX_i \} , \qquad\qquad (3-7)$$

where ($XMIN_i$, $XMAX_i$, $YMIN_i$, $YMAX_i$) denotes the MBR of the i-th old region.

(3) Scatter matrix --- Let C_i, M_i, and S_i (i=1...n) denote respectively the scatter matrix, the position vector of the mass center, and the area of the i-th old region. Let M denote the position vector of the mass center of the new region, which is calculated by equation 3-6. Then the new scatter matrix C can be obtained as follows:

$$C = (\sum_{i=1}^{N} S_i \ (C_i + (M_i - M)(M_i - M)^t)) / \sum_{i=1}^{N} S_i . \qquad\qquad (3-8)$$

Table 3-2. Secondary features which can be derived
from the primary ones.

features of a region	normalized colors; intensity; saturation; hue; compactness; VH-ratio (crude shape); effective width; effective MBR.
features between two regions	contrast of the border; orientation of the border; linearity of the border; T-ratio (touching ratio); O-ratio (overlapping ratio); placement relations (above, below, etc.).

3.4.2. Derivation of various features

Various kinds of features are used in region analysis systems to represent the properties of and the relations between the regions. Table 3-2 shows the typical features which are actually used. We will show how one can derive these secondary features easily from the primary ones entered in the Patchery Data Structure. The computational time necessary to derive them from the data structure is less than that required to compute them directly from the image arrays.

(1) Normalized colors (r, g, and b), intensity, hue, and saturation of a region --- These can be calculated from the mean intensities of R, G, and B of the region.

$$r = R/(R+G+B), \quad g = G/(R+G+B), \quad b = B/(R+G+B),$$
$$\text{intensity} = (R+G+B)/3,$$
$$\text{saturation} = 1 - 3 \times \min(r,g,b),$$
$$\text{hue} = \arctan2(3^{1/2}(G-B),(2R-G-B)) \ . \tag{3-9}$$

(2) Compactness of a region --- This can be calculated from the area and the contour length of a region.

$$\text{compactness} = 4\pi(\text{area})/(\text{contour length})^2 \ . \tag{3-10}$$

(3) Crude shapes of a region such as vertically-long or horizontally-long --- These can be defined based on the VH-ratio, which is computed using the scatter matrix.

$$\text{VH-ratio} = \log(C_{11}/C_{22}) \ , \tag{3-11}$$

where C_{11} and C_{22} are the diagonal components of the scatter matrix C.

(4) Effective width and effective MBR of a region --- The effective width and the effective MBR are both computed from the scatter matrix. When the scatter matrix of a region is $\begin{pmatrix} C11 & C12 \\ C21 & C22 \end{pmatrix}$, the effective MBR (XMIN, XMAX, YMIN, YMAX) is a rectangle which has a scatter matrix $\begin{pmatrix} C11 & 0 \\ 0 & C22 \end{pmatrix}$. The

effective width (XW, YW) is the width of the effective MBR.

$$XW = 2(3C_{11})^{1/2}, \qquad YW = 2(3C_{22})^{1/2},$$
$$XMIN = XC-XW/2, \qquad XMAX = XC+XW/2,$$
$$YMIN = YC-YW/2, \qquad YMAX = YC+YW/2, \qquad\qquad (3-12)$$

where (XC, YC) is the mass center of the region.

(5) The contrast at the border of two regions --- This can be computed by averaging the contrast of the boundary segments included in the intersection of the contours of the two regions.

(6) The degree that a region touches another region (T-ratio) --- The T-ratio of region-1 to region-2 is calculated from the length of the border between the two regions and the contour length of region-1.

$$\text{T-ratio} = (border\ length)/(contour\ length\ of\ region-1). \qquad (3-13)$$

(7) The degree of a region being surrounded by another region (O-ratio) --- The O-ratio of region-1 to region-2 is computed as the ratio of the overlapped area of the MBRs of the two regions to the whole area of the MBR of region-1.

$$\text{O-ratio} = (overlapped\ area)/(whole\ area\ of\ region-1's\ MBR). \qquad (3-14)$$

(8) The linearity and the orientation of the border between two regions --- These can be derived from the set of line segments included in the boundary of the two regions.

(9) Positional relationships between two regions such as above, below, left, or right --- These can be derived by using the mass centers and the MBRs of the two regions. Let (XC_1, YC_1) and (XC_2, YC_2) be the mass centers of region-1 and region-2, respectively. Let $(XMIN_1, XMAX_1, YMIN_1, YMAX_1)$ and $(XMIN_2, XMAX_2, YMIN_2, YMAX_2)$ be the effective MBRs of the two regions illustrated in figure 3-16. Then the relation "region-1 is above region-2" is defined as follows:

66

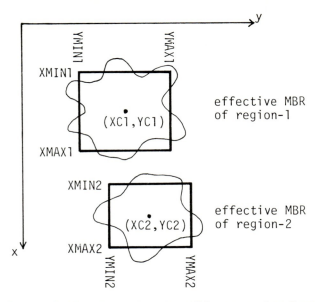

Figure 3-16.   Two effective MBRs to define "above".

$$XMIN_1 < (XMIN_2+XC_2)/2 \wedge XMAX_1 < XC_2 \wedge YMIN_2 < YC_1 < YMAX_2. \qquad (3\text{-}15)$$

Actually, we defined "above" as a fuzzy predicate; the truth value is affected by the degree that YC_1 is out of the range $[YMIN_2, YMAX_2]$. The other relations are defined in the same way.

3.4.3. Retrieving the regions

When the analysis is performed by means of a top-down strategy, it is necessary to retrieve regions by specifying the properties they should have; for example, "fetch all the regions that are long vertically and have a yellow region on their left". Such a retrieval usually needs a very large computation. Only a well-structured symbolic description can allow such a function to be of practical use. In our system, the following three primitive functions are for this purpose (cf. table 4-3).

ALL-FETCH (to-set, from-set, fuzzy-predicate) ,

THERE-IS (region, from-set, fuzzy-predicate) ,

T-FETCH (to-set, region) .

```
(ALL-FETCH  *TO-SET  *REGIONS
    (AND  (VERTICALLY-LONG  *TO-SET)
          (THERE-IS  *Y-RGN  *REGIONS
             (AND  (YELLOW  *Y-RGN)
                   (LEFT-OF  *Y-RGN  *TO-SET)))))))
```

Figure 3-17. The function to "fetch all regions that are long
vertically and have a yellow region on their left".

ALL-FETCH selects from a set of regions, which is specified by from-set,
all the regions that satisfy the condition described by fuzzy-predicate, and
assigns them to to-set. THERE-IS (an existential fetch) selects only the one
region found first. Nested use of these functions realizes arbitrarily
complicated retrievals. T-FETCH selects all the regions that are touching
region. This function, of course, can be realized by using ALL-FETCH, but
T-FETCH is faster because it utilizes the relational pointers in the Patchery
Data Structure. Figure 3-17 illustrates a function defined by using ALL-FETCH
and THERE-IS to perform the retrieval of the above example, "fetch all the
regions that are ...".

3.5. The Results

The segmentation process and the structuring process described in this
chapter have been applied to a number of color scenes, and have produced
successful results. This section presents the results for two scenes for
illustration. Other results can be seen in appendix A.

Figure 3-18-a is an outdoor scene. The input picture is digitized with
256×256 size and 5-bit density resolution for each R, G, and B data. Figure
3-18-b shows the result of segmentation. R, G, and B are used as the color
features for histogramming in the segmentation algorithm. The detailed
structures, such as the windows of the building, are extracted successfully.
Fragmentation of the textural parts like trees is suppressed. Conceivably, the
quality of this segmentation is sufficient as the "nonpurposive" segmentation.

(a) digitized image

(b) result of segmentation

(c) straight line segments

(d) reconstructed image

Figure 3-18. Result of preliminary segmentation: Example 1.

(a) digitized image

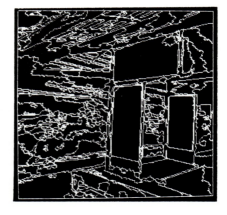

(b) result of segmentation

(c) straight line segments

(d) reconstructed image

Figure 3-19. Result of preliminary segmentation: Example 2.

Figure 3-18-c shows the straight line segments fit on the boundary segments. Figure 3-18-d is a color image reconstructed from the structured description finally obtained. Mean intensity values of R, G, and B are assigned to each region. In this example the number of regions is 339, the number of boundary segments is 914, the number of vertices is 612, the number of holes is 37, and the number of line segments is 268. The storage necessary for this data structure is about 90K bytes.

Figure 3-19 shows the result of another color scene. In this case, the input picture is digitized with 256×256 size and 6-bit density resolution. Three color features (R+G+B)/3, (R-B), and (2G-R-B)/2 are used in the segmentation process. The numbers of regions, boundary segments, vertices, holes, and line segments are 391, 1121, 742, 11, and 368, respectively.

3.6. Conclusion

In this chapter, a system which computes a structured description of a color image based on regions is described. A powerful segmentation process has been developed by improving the segmentation algorithm, which uses multihistograms to obtain the cues for splitting a region. The segmentation results are organized into a structured symbolic data network. It contains a rich description of the input image and supplies the analysis process with the pictorial information in a tractable form.

The features of the system are as follows.

For the segmentation process:
 (1)   It can deal with color images.
 (2)   The global structures in the input image are effectively extracted by using histograms as the cues for segmentation.
 (3)   The detailed structures can be extracted by the window-scanning method.
 (4)   The meaningless fragmentation of the textural area in the input scene is avoided by the pre-extraction of that area.
 (5)   It works well for various kinds of images.

As for the structured description:
 (6)   Because it is region-based, the properties such as colors or textural features can be described in a natural way.
 (7)   The features entered in the description are limited to the primary ones. This results in a relatively small size for the description.

(8) Various kinds of features can be derived efficiently from the description.

(9) Region fetch functions, which retrieve regions satisfying certain properties from the input image, can be realized on the description.

(10) Merging operations on the regions can be performed using the description without referring to the image arrays.

There are a few unsolved problems. First, our description cannot support the splitting operation on regions. This problem, however, can be almost avoided by over-segmenting the image in the segmentation process. Secondly, the segmentation process takes a lot of time. This can be substantially improved by employing special purpose hardware which can perform high-speed parallel computation for low-level operations such as histogramming and thresholding.

Figure 2−17 (a)
(See page 38.)

Figure 2−17 (b)
(See page 38.)

Figure 2−18 (a)
(See page 39.)

Figure 2−18 (b)
(See page 39.)

Figure 2−19 (a)
(See page 40.)

Figure 2−19 (b)
(See page 40.)

Figure 2−20 (a)
(See page 41.)

Figure 2−20 (b)
(See page 41.)

Figure 4−11 (a)
(See page 104.)

Figure 4−13 (a)
(See page 107.)

Figure 4−15 (a)
(See page 110.)

4 A Bottom-up and Top-down Region Analyzer

4.1. The Problems

Region analysis techniques are often employed in analysis systems for natural scenes. A region analyzer tries to segment an input image into meaningful regions and assigns object labels to each of them. The term "meaningful" means that each region corresponds to a part of a surface of one of the objects in the input scene. The homogeneity of color or texture is used as the criteria for dividing the image into regions. A meaningful segmentation, however, is hardly ever achieved by using only such image properties. Various kinds of additional constraints must be employed to obtain the meaningful regions.

Brice et al. [1970] segmented blocks-world scenes by the region growing technique. They employed the "phagocyte" heuristic in addition to the "weakness" heuristic which evaluates the similarity of brightness. That is, even if the boundary between two regions is weak, they are joined only if the resulting boundary does not grow too fast. Thus, the phagocyte heuristic constrains the region growing process to obtain well-shaped regions. It worked well for the block scenes.

For more complex scenes such as outdoor scenes, it is necessary to introduce more task-specific constraints into the segmentation process. Yakimovsky et al. [1973] incorporated the interpretation process into the segmentation process, and analyzed road scenes which included sky, roads, grass strips, trees, and cars. The input image was first divided into small fragments based on similarity of color. Every fragment was interpreted by using the properties of and the relations between the fragments. The fragments which were assigned an identical interpretation were merged as a single meaningful region. Their scheme utilized the restrictions on the kinds of objects in the task world as constraints to guide the segmentation. Tenenbaum et al. [1976] analyzed a room scene by a method which they called "Interpretation-Guided Segmentation". These two methods are usually called "semantic region analysis".

The semantic region analysis systems have succeeded in analyzing road scenes and simple room scenes. But they cannot deal with scenes which contain objects for whose recognition a certain structure has to be identified. For example, it is difficult to deal with a set of regions, such as windows of a building, which are located separately, but which are to be identified as a whole according to some placement rules. The evaluation of shapes comprising several regions is also hard. The reason for this difficulty can be understood as follows. The semantic region analysis technique has been developed as an improvement of the region growing technique. Thus, it still relies entirely on the bottom-up control scheme of the region growing process, and the semantic information is used in the same way as the local pictorial information. Consequently, even though the segmentation is evaluated by a certain score, the usable features which evaluate the semantic constraints are limited to local ones: e.g. color, orientation of a boundary segment, crude shape of a boundary segment, etc. Such a problem stems from the fact that the semantic region analyses so far developed are based on the bottom-up control scheme.

In order to resolve the problem, a model-driven top-down approach seems essential. It is well known that, when the structure of the input scene is known, the top-down control scheme provides an efficient and reliable analysis. Under top-down control, it becomes possible to deal with a set of regions located separately in the image such as windows of a building. But when the structure is not known, the top-down scheme is powerless. In contrast, the bottom-up control is usually not so efficient, but it is more robust; it works well even when the structure of the input image is not known. We think that we can build a powerful analysis mechanism by combining the merits of the two complementary control schemes in the following way: (1) The bottom-up control scheme extracts information about the crude structure of the input scene. (2) Based on the information provided by the bottom-up analysis, the top-down control scheme performs an efficient analysis by focussing its attention.

The task world selected is campus scenes of Kyoto University; the scenes include sky, trees, buildings, roads, windows of buildings, and cars on roads.

4.2. A Bottom-up and Top-down Region Analyzer

4.2.1. Patches and regions

Figure 4-1 shows the outline of our region analyzer. An input color image is first partitioned into a set of coherent regions according to the color information. The partition is performed to the state of over-segmentation, that is, we can assume a single region does not span more than one object, but one object might be divided into multiple regions. The segmented image is organized into a structured data network which is called the Patchery Data Structure. Regions, boundary segments, vertices, holes, and (straight) line segments are used as the descriptive elements. This prccess is called the preliminary segmentation.

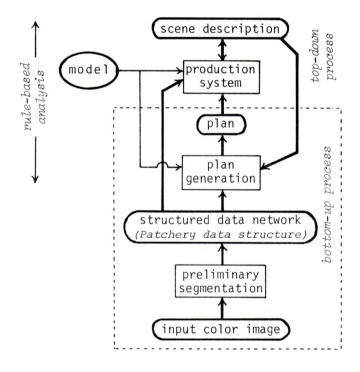

Figure 4-1. Outline of the region analyzer.

After this, coherent regions obtained in the preliminary segmentation are denoted by the term "patches". The term "regions" is used only for the regions which are obtained by merging the patches according to a certain criterion. The patches are the input to the rule-based region analyzer and are the atomic elements used to construct a scene description.

4.2.2. Bottom-up control and top-down control

Deciding where to locate the interface between the bottom-up and top-down processes is an important problem. In figure 4-1, the part enclosed by dotted lines is performed under bottom-up control in our system. A "plan" is generated by the bottom-up process as a representation of the crude structure of the input scene. The plan is a set of object labels and their degree of correctness, assigned to each of the large patches in the preliminarily segmented image. The plan provides the top-down process with the clues concerning what knowledge can be applied to what part of the scene.

The top-down process, referring to the plan generated in the bottom-up process, fixes the interpretation for the large patches. Also, it analyzes the detailed structures of the scene by interpreting small patches in the context of the large patches which have been already interpreted. When the top-down process makes a significant decision (such as the position of the scene horizon) which might have an effect on the interpretation of the whole scene, tne decision is fed back to the bottom-up process and the plan is re-evaluated. In this way the bottom-up process and the top-down process work cooperatively to construct the semantic description of the scene.

4.2.3. Rule-based analysis

Knowledge of the task world is represented by two sets of rules in our region analyzer: one set is used in the bottom-up process and the other in the top-down process. Figure 4-2 illustrates the control mechanism of the region analyzer. Because the knowledge is represented as a collection of modular rules, it is easy to add or modify the knowledge in our system. This is a useful feature in organizing an analysis system for complex scenes, such as outdoor scenes, which include various kinds of objects.

Each rule for the bottom-up process has a fuzzy predicate which describes properties of or relations between objects. It also has a weight which indicates the uncertainty of the knowledge it relies on. The plan manager controls

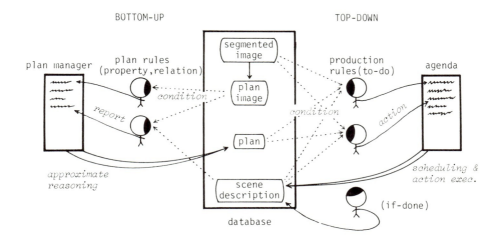

BOTTOM-UP TOP-DOWN

Figure 4-2. Control mechanism of the rule-based analysis.

evaluation of the rules and performs an approximate reasoning based on the fuzzy truth values. Section 4-3 describes this in detail.

The top-down process is organized as a production system. Each rule is a condition-action pair. The condition is a fuzzy predicate which examines the situation of the database. The action includes operations to construct the scene description. An agenda manages the activation of production rules and schedules the executable actions. A detailed description can be found in section 4-4.

4.2.4. Plan generation by bottom-up analysis

Plan image   In order to generate the plan, patches with large area are first selected from the segmented image. It is reasonable to assume that most of them correspond to large parts of objects in the scene and that they can be extracted from the image data rather stably in the segmentation process. We call those patches keypatches. It should be possible to grasp the rough structure of the scene by assigning the object labels to the keypatches. The labels have multiple

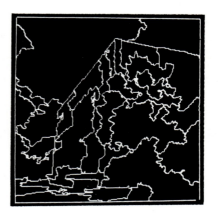

(a) result of preliminary   (b) plan image generated
    segmentation   from (a)

Figure 4-3.   Generation of a plan image.

values, and a score indicating the degree of correctness is associated with each
label value; for example,

        label-of-a-keypatch = [(sky=0.5)(building=0.2)(tree=0.2)(road=0.1)].

The score is computed by evaluating the properties of and the relations between
the keypatches.

        Small patches in the segmented image may disturb the evaluation of the
relations between the keypatches.   Thus, we tentatively merge all the small
patches with one of the keypatches. We call the resultant image a "plan image".
The "plan" is the labeled plan image;   that is, each region in the plan image is
assigned a label.

        Figure 4-3-b shows the plan image generated from the segmented image in
figure 4-3-a. Note that the plan image is represented symbolically in the
Patchery Data Structure, and the image (2-D array) in figure 4-3-b is generated
only for the purpose of display.

78

No semantic information is used in the merge operation. When a small patch touches more than two keypatches, a score is computed for each keypatch based on the similarity of color and the compactness of the region which would be obtained if the small patch and the keypatch were merged. The compactness criterion guides the merging operation to obtain regions with smooth boundaries. In order to evaluate the global relations between regions, smooth boundaries are rather convenient. The keypatch which obtains the highest score is selected. The merge operation is, of course, performed by manipulating the Patchery Data Structure.

Rules and plan manager   Each rule used in the plan generation process has a fuzzy predicate which describes a property of a certain object or a relation between objects. When a rule is applied to a region to check whether the region can be labeled as an object, it examines pictorial features of the region and produces a fuzzy truth-value which indicates the degree of satisfaction of the property. The predicate can also examine the scene description which is constructed in the top-down process. In this way, the information extracted in the top-down process, such as the position of the scene horizon, can be reflected in the plan generation process.

In order to evaluate the plan, the plan manager activates every rule to examine every region in the plan image. For every combination of rules and regions, the plan manager receives a fuzzy truth-value. Based on the set of fuzzy truth-values, the plan manager assigns object labels to each of the regions and computes their degrees of correctness.

An approximate reasoning scheme is employed for evaluation of the plan to deal with the uncertainty existing in both the knowledge and the pictorial features. Detailed description of this scheme is included in section 4-3.

4.2.5. Top-down analysis of patches

A production system architecture   The top-down analysis process uses a production system architecture. A production system consists of a set of production rules, a database, and a control structure. A production rule is the unit of knowledge representation, and the database records the facts about the input image. Each production rule is a condition-action pair, and is "watching" the database. Whenever the predicate in the condition part is satisfied, the system evaluates the action part and modifies the database.

As illustrated in figure 4-2, the database stores

(1) the preliminarily segmented image and the plan image represented in the Patchery Data Structure,

(2) the plan, and

(3) the scene description so far obtained.

There are two types of production rules in our system: to-do rules and if-done rules. They correspond to the consequent and antecedent theorems of PLANNER [Hewitt, 1968], respectively. A to-do rule performs basic operations in the region analysis process. The fuzzy predicate in its condition part examines each patch in the segmented image which has not yet been interpreted, and determines whether the associated action can be executed. The executable action-patch pairs are added into the agenda with scores indicating their priorities, whose computation will be explained soon. The agenda controls the production system. It manages action-patch pairs which are executable at each point of analysis. The pair with the highest score is executed and, as the result, the agenda is updated.

An if-done rule is a demon. It is triggered by the execution of a certain action of to-do rules. A rule which activates the re-evaluation of plan when a label is assigned to a keypatch is a typical example of an if-done rule.

In the production system architecture, interactions of the to-do rules and if-done rules as they modify the database embody a heterarchical control structure. This enables the top-down analysis process to have a flavor of data-driven control so that the order of analysis is determined according to the reliability of the interpretation of each part of the image, which is given as the plan generated by the bottom-up analysis.

Structure of scene description   Well-organized description of analysis results is essential for realizing an effective top-down control scheme. That is, the system must be able to grasp the current status exactly to control the analysis process. Figure 4-4 illustrates the structure of the scene description which is built as the result of the top-down analysis in our system. Scene, object, region, sub-region, patch, and pixel are the important concepts which constitute the structure of the description.

The patches are the ones obtained as the output of the preliminary segmentation. They are the atomic elements in the rule-based analysis. The scene represents the whole image being analyzed. The objects stand for the objects extracted from the scene. The regions represent the main parts of objects such

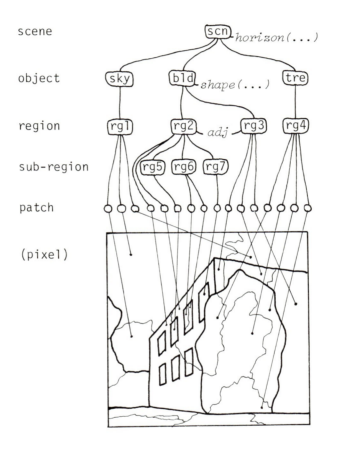

scene

object

region

sub-region

patch

(pixel)

Figure 4-4. Structure of the scene description.

as the walls of buildings, and they are obtained by merging the patches which
are given the same interpretation. The sub-regions are much the same as the
regions, but they correspond to subjective parts of objects such as the windows
of buildings. The difference between (sub-)regions and patches is that the
former are the entities given consistent semantic interpretation, whereas the
latter are the entities having consistent pictorial properties. All descriptive
elements are organized into a hierarchical structure by the "part-of" relation.
Relations between the objects, such as "adjacent" or "occluding", are described
between corresponding regions.

4.3. Modeling and Control Structure for Plan Generation

4.3.1. Model representation

Knowledge block organization of model   In a computer vision system, a model
which describes the properties of and the relations between the objects is the
most important knowledge representation about the task world. In our system, the
model is organized as a semantic network as illustrated in figure 4-5. Each node
of the network is called a knowledge block in our model. It holds a chunk of
knowledge about an entity in the world; for instance, object "sky", material
"concrete", property "blue", relation "linear-boundary", etc. A knowledge block
for an object or material includes a set of rules which describe properties it
must satisfy and relations it has with other blocks, and a set of production
rules which belong to it. A knowledge block for a property or relation includes
its definition.

The most valuable advantage of our representation over an ordinary semantic
network is that it has a mechanism with which to represent both the universal
knowledge, such as property inheritance from material to object, and the
"active" rules, such as the production rules, that the interpretation process
can use in a specific context of analysis.

Rules describing properties and relations   The knowledge block for an object
or material holds the description of the properties which must be satisfied by a
region corresponding to that object or material. It also holds the description
of the relations which must be satisfied between the regions corresponding to
that object and other objects. The properties and the relations are represented
as a set of declarative rules of the following formats.

82

```
property: [(<type><fuzzy-predicate><weight>)(<var-list>)]
relation: [(<type><fuzzy-predicate><weight> FOR <label>)(<var-list>)]
```

The <fuzzy-predicate> defines the property or the relation itself. Its syntax is as much the same as the "form" in Lisp language. Figure 4-6 shows the syntax defined by the BNF notation. Some explanatory examples are given later in this section.

The <var-list> is a list of external variables used in the fuzzy predicate. There is exactly one variable in the <var-list> of property rules and two in relation rules. The control program binds each of the external variables to the regions (or patches) which must be examined by the predicate. The fuzzy predicate evaluates the property of the region or the relation between the two regions, and returns a fuzzy truth-value.

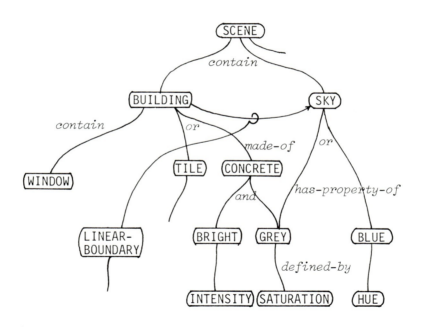

Figure 4-5.   A semantic network for knowledge organization.

The <weight> is a dotted pair of two numbers ($W_1.W_2$). It indicates the uncertainty of the knowledge the rule relies on. Let A be the property represented by the rule, and let X be the object to which the rule belongs. Then the first number W_1 corresponds to the a priori probability P[A] that a region satisfies the property A. W_2 corresponds to the conditional probability P[A!X] that a region known to be the object X satisfies the property A.

The <type> discriminates types of knowledge the rule relies on. There are two types: GEN (GENeral) and STR (STeReotyped). The GEN-type rule corresponds to a general type of knowledge, such as "sky is blue or grey". The STR-type rule represents the knowledge about a stereotype, such as "the region which touches the lower side of the picture frame may be a part of road"; of course, we cannot

```
<fuzzy predicate>::=<constant>|<variable>|
                    (<function name><arguments>)
<arguments>::=<empty>|<argument><arguments>
<argument>::=<fuzzy predicate>
<function name>::=<block name>|<subroutine name>
<block name>::=*<letter><letters>
<subroutine name>::=<letter><letters>
<variable>::=<block name>
<constant>::=<letter><letters>|<number><numbers>|
             <number><numbers>.<number><numbers>
<numbers>::=<empty>|<number><numbers>
<letters>::=<empty>|<letter><letters>|<number><letters>
<number>::=0|1|2|...
<letter>::=A|B|C|...
```

Figure 4-6. Syntax of fuzzy predicates.
    A <block name> used as a <argument> is a <variable>.
    A <letter><letters> used as a <argument> is a <constant>.
    A <block name> used as a <function name> corresponds to
    a <fuzzy predicate> whose definition is described in
    the model.

84

say that a region is not a part of road unless it touches the lower side. The difference between the two types is not very essential. But, this taxonomy is helpful in making the rules and in determining the weight values.

The <label> specifies the object with which the relation should hold.

The following are typical examples of the property rules and the relation rules.

(a) A property rule in the knowledge block "sky";

knowledge: The sky is blue or grey.

rule   : [(GEN (OR (*BLUE *SK)(*GREY *SK)) (1.0 . 0.2)) (*SK)]

(b) A relation rule in the knowledge block "building";

knowledge: The boundary between the building and the sky has a
           lot of linear parts, and the building is not on the
           upper side of that boundary.

rule   : [(GEN (AND (*LINEAR-BOUNDARY *BL *SK)
                     (NOT (POSITION UP *BL *SK)))
               (1.0 . 0.5) FOR SKY) (*BL *SK)]

Definition of fuzzy predicates   We defined various pictorial properties such as "green", "grey", "textural", etc. as fuzzy predicates in the model. Those predicates are defined by using the corresponding pictorial features. For instance, "green" is defined by the feature "hue", "grey" by "saturation", and "textural" by "degree of texture". We use three functions, FUZZY1, FUZZY2, and FUZZY3, to map the pictorial feature values onto the fuzzy truth-values. Figure 4-7 illustrates the mapping schemes. FUZZY1 and FUZZY2 have four arguments. The first one is the pictorial feature. The second and third ones are the thresholds T_1 and T_2 which are shown in figure 4-7. Pictorial features taking values between T_1 and T_2 are mapped onto fuzzy truth-values between the minimum and maximum truth-values. The fourth argument is used to reflect the uncertainty of the pictorial feature to the fuzzy truth-value. Let us consider the fuzzy predicate *GREY for "grey". When the color of a region is very dark, its saturation is unreliable. In such a case, the fuzzy truth-value must be 0.5, which means "nothing is said about the property 'grey'", regardless of its saturation. Then FUZZY1 and FUZZY2 adjust their maximum and minimum truth-values according to the fuzzy truth-value given in its fourth argument.

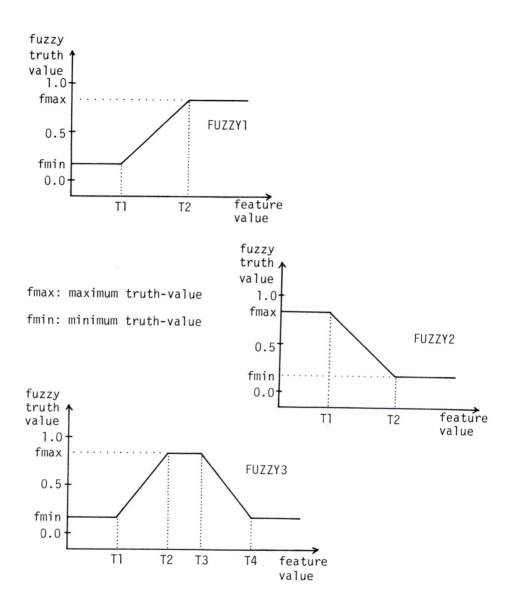

fmax: maximum truth-value

fmin: minimum truth-value

Figure 4-7.   Three functions to define truth-value of
fuzzy predicates from the feature value.

```
maximum truth-value = 0.5+(value of the fourth argument)/2 ,
minimum truth-value = 0.5-(value of the fourth argument)/2 .        (4-1)
```

When the fourth argument is omitted, the maximum and minimum truth-values are defaulted to 1.0 and 0.0, respectively. The function FUZZY3 has two more arguments: the thresholds T_3 and T_4 (see figure 4-7).

The followings are explanatory examples of fuzzy-predicate definitions.

```
textural:  [(*X)(FUZZY1 (TEXTURE-DEGREE *X) 1.0 4.0 (*BRIGHT *X))]
grey:      [(*X)(FUZZY2 (SATURATION *X) 0.05 0.15 (*BRIGHT *X))]
green:     [(*X)(FUZZY3 (HUE *X) 0.5 1.0 2.5 3.0 (NOT (*GREY *X)))]
```

4.3.2. Evaluation of plan

The evaluation of the plan means the evaluation of the degree of correctness of the labels assigned to each region in the plan image. In order to evaluate the plan, the plan manager activates the rules for plan generation to examine the regions in the plan image. Three numbers are used to compute the degree of correctness of a label assigned to a region. They are (1) the a priori probability of the label, (2) the results of the property rules evaluated with the region, and (3) the results of the relation rules evaluated between the region and other regions; these numbers are used in this order. The a priori probability given in the model for each object label is used as the base value of the degree of correctness. First, the property rules are used to revise the correctness values. Then, the relation rules are used for further revision. This is because the evaluation of a relation can take place only after the labels of the partner regions are assigned with some confidence.

Calculation of revision factor   According to the Bayes rule of conditional probabilities, the following equation 4-2 holds. Let $P[X_m]$ be the a priori probability that a label X_m matches with a region. Let $P[X_m|A]$ be the posteriori probability that a label X_m matches with a region after a property A is observed with the region. Let $P[A]$ denote the a priori probability that a region satisfies the property A. Let $P[A|X_m]$ be the conditional probability that a region with the label X_m satisfies the property A:

$$P[X_m|A] = P[X_m] * P[A|X_m]/P[A] .$$ (4-2)

In our region analysis, Equation 4-2 can be interpreted as follows: when a region Q_i satisfies a fuzzy-predicate-A in a property rule R_{mk},

[(<type> fuzzy-predicate-A <weight>) (<var-list>)],

the correctness value of the label X_m for the region Q_i can be $P[A|X_m]/P[A]$ times reinforced. Recall that the numbers $P[A|X_m]$ and $P[A]$ are given as the <weight> in the rule R_{mk}.

Let T_{imk} be the fuzzy truth-value of the fuzzy-predicate-A in the rule R_{mk} evaluated for the region Q_i. T_{imk} takes a value of the range [0, 1]; T_{imk} equal to 1 or 0 means that the fuzzy predicate is or is not satisfied totally; T_{imk} between 0 and 1 means that the satisfaction is ambiguous; T_{imk} equal to 0.5 means that nothing is said about the existence of the property. Then, it is necessary to adjust the revision of the correctness value C_{im} according to the value of T_{imk}. For this purpose, a revision factor F_{imk} is derived from the $P[A|X_m]$, $P[A]$, and T_{imk}. The C_{im} is revised by multiplying F_{imk} instead of $P[A|X_m]/P[A]$. Figure 4-8 shows the relation of revision factor vs. fuzzy truth-value.

For the GEN-type rule when the fuzzy truth-value T_{imk} is 1 or 0 (i.e., the property either does or does not exist totally), the correctness value C_{im} becomes $P[A|X_m]/P[A]$ or $P[\bar{A}|X_m]/P[\bar{A}]$ times reinforced or weakened. When T_{imk} is 0.5 (i.e., nothing is said about the property), the C_{im} does not change at all ($F_{imk}=1$). For the STR-type rule, the correctness value C_{im} is kept unchanged when the property is not recognized, i.e. $F_{imk}=1$ for $T_{imk} \le 0.5$.

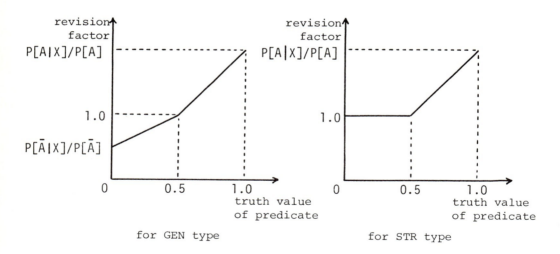

Figure 4-8.   Relation of the revision factor vs. the
fuzzy truth-value.

Evaluation of property rules   In general, there are multiple property rules describing the properties which must be satisfied by a region with label X_m. Let K_m be the number of the property rules for the label X_m. The computation of a correctness value is performed sequentially; it is revised as the rules are evaluated one by one. Let F_{imk} ($k=1...K_m$) be the revision factor obtained by evaluating the k-th property rule R_{mk} for a region Q_i. Let C_{im}^0 be the correctness value of the label X_m for the region Q_i after evaluating all the property rules (the relation rules have not been used yet). Then C_{im}^0 is calculated by

$$C_{im}^0 = (P[X_m] * \prod_{k=1}^{Km} F_{imk}) / \sum_{m=1}^{M} (P[X_m] * \prod_{k=1}^{Km} F_{imk}), \tag{4-3}$$

where $P[X_m]$ is the a priori probability of the label X_m.

Notice that equation 4-3 includes the normalization of C_{im}^0 such that $\sum_{m=1}^{M} C_{im}^0 = 1$, where M is the number of labels (objects) in the model.

Above process assumes the statistical independence of property rules as MYCIN does [Shortliffe, 1976]. While the assumption may not be true, it is necessary to maintain the modularity of each rule.

Evaluation of relation rules   The correctness value C_{im}^0 is now revised by evaluating the relation rules R_{mnk} ($k=1...K_{mn}$) which describe the relations between a region with label X_m and another region with label X_n. Let T_{imjnk} be the fuzzy truth-value obtained by evaluating the k-th rule R_{mnk} for a region Q_i with the label X_m and a region Q_j with the label X_n. Then the correctness value C_{im} of the label X_m for the region Q_i can be revised by multiplying the revision factor F_{imjnk} which is calculated from T_{imjnk} and the weight of the rule R_{mnk}. But the situation is a little different from the case of property rules. The correctness value C_{jn} of the label X_n in the region Q_j must be considered. Actually, C_{jn} takes a 0-to-1 value. When C_{jn} is near 0, the evaluation of the rule R_{mnk} between the regions Q_i and Q_j makes no sense. Then, the revision factor F_{imjnk} must be adjusted according to the value of C_{jn}, as well as T_{imjnk}, when revising the correctness value C_{im}. Equation 4-4 defines the computation of C_{im}.

$$C_{im} = C_{im}^0 * \prod_{j=1}^{J} \prod_{n=1}^{N} \prod_{k=1}^{K_{mn}} \{(F_{imjnk}-1) * C_{jn} + 1\} , \tag{4-4}$$

where J is the number of regions in the plan image,

N is the number of labels in the model,

K_{mn} is the number of relation rules described

between the labels X_m and X_n.

The revision is performed for all pairs of the region Q_i and other regions Q_j in the plan image, for all labels X_n in Q_j, and for all relation rules between the labels X_m and X_n. The C_{jn} in the right side of equation 4-4 is also revised by evaluating the relation rules. Then we would need to solve J × N equations to obtain the exact values of C_{im} (i=1...J and m=1...N). Here, we employed the relaxation method to solve the equation approximately. Let C_{im}^h be the value of C_{im} after the h-th iteration. C_{im}^h's are computed by the successive use of equation 4-5.

$$C_{im}^h = C_{im}^0 * \prod_{j=1}^{J} \prod_{n=1}^{N} \prod_{k=1}^{K_{mn}} \{(F_{imjnk}-1) * C_{jn}(h-1)+1\} ,$$

$$(i=1...J \text{ and } m=1...N) . \tag{4-5}$$

The initial values for C_{jn}^{h-1} are C_{jn}^0 which are the correctness values obtained by using the property rules. When C_{im}^0 or C_{jn}^{h-1} is small, the values of F_{imjnk} are not sufficiently reflected to the revision of the C_{im}. This means the evaluation of relation rules to obtain F_{imjnk}'s in such a situation does not pay much from the computational point of view. In our system, F_{imjnk} is evaluated only when $C_{im}^0 \geq$ 0.1 and $C_{jn}^{h-1} \geq$ 0.5. Consequently, the number of relation rules which need to be actually evaluated is rather small, and the computation of equation 4-5 becomes feasible. Two or three iterations of equation 4-5 are enough to produce approximate solutions of C_{im}.

4.4. A Production System for Region Analysis

4.4.1. Representing knowledge by production rules

When we import the production system architecture to image analysis, it is an important problem to determine the "size" of knowledge which can be represented by one production rule. An example of "large" knowledge size is a system in which each production rule corresponds to one object to be extracted and has complete knowledge about the object. This enables the system to perform a skillful analysis according to the characteristics of each object. On the other hand, the rules become large and complex, which makes them difficult to manage.

In our system the size of knowledge represented by a single rule is fairly small. Each rule describes a combination of basic operations for region analysis: selecting a patch which has not yet been interpreted from the segmented image, assigning a label to it, and assembling it into the scene description. This scheme has the following merits: Each rule is simple and easy to write and modify; and the interaction among rules is clear because the access method to the database is uniform.

On the other hand, the patch-by-patch analysis in our scheme gives rise to a certain difficulty in dealing with global constraints such as object shapes or relations among objects. We take three steps to resolve this difficulty. First, we generate a plan as a rough interpretation of the input scene. The plan is put into the database and each production rule can freely access it. This allows the production rules to gain information about global structures of the scene. Second, a set of patches can be dealt with at one time, as well as individual patches, and it becomes possible to extract an object which is defined as a combination of mutually constrained patches, such as the windows of a building or a car on a road. Finally, we have devised special rules which extract information from the segmented image without sticking to the patch-by-patch analysis. Typically, this kind of rule is used to extract the shape of a building.

4.4.2. Control structure

Scene phase and object phase   Conceptually, each production rule in the production system architecture concurrently checks the status of the database, and executes the associated action when its condition is satisfied. Actually, however, the control program examines one by one every pair of production rules and patches which have not been interpreted yet. The pair which seems to give the most reliable interpretation is selected for execution. An agenda is used to schedule the executable pairs at any moment in the analysis. The agenda must be updated whenever the database is changed. Roughly speaking, the number of tests to be done each time is estimated as

number of tests = (the number of un-interpreted patches)

$$\times \text{ (the number of production rules),} \qquad (4\text{-}6)$$

which can easily become several thousand tests. Testing them all is computationally unfeasible.

It is necessary to reduce the number of the patches and production rules which must be actually examined at a time. For this, the structure of scenes must be considered.

A scene usually has two different properties from the point of view of image analysis: "Globality" and "Locality". Results of analysis such as the determination of scene horizon or the detection of objects can have significant influence on the analysis of the overall structure of the scene. This property is called "Globality". On the other hand, results of analysis in a small part of an object scarcely influences the analysis of other parts in the scene. This property is called "Locality".

These two properties are effectively utilized in the control structure of our scene analyzer. In accordance with the two properties, the control program works in two phases: scene phase and object phase. The scene phase is for analyzing the overall structure of the input scene without attending to details. Since it is almost meaningless to examine small patches in this scene phase, only the keypatches are examined. Whenever a keypatch is labeled, the agenda activates the scene phase and all keypatches that have not yet been labeled are re-examined. In the object phase, the analysis of detailed structures proceeds under the context of the results in the scene phase. When a patch which belongs to an object is labeled, the agenda activates the object phase corresponding to that object, and those patches touching the patch just labeled are examined or re-examined.

The set of production rules can be divided into subsets to be used in the scene phase and the object phase. The production rules for the object phase are further divided into subsets corresponding to each object. In each phase, only the production rules in appropriate subsets are activated by the agenda to examine the patches which have not yet been interpreted.

Consequently, the number of tests to be done at a time is reduced to several 10s.

Control structure   The control structure of our production system is simple. Basically, the analysis iterates the following three steps.

1. An executable action registered on the agenda is selected and executed. A patch or a set of patches is interpreted, and the database is modified. If the agenda has no executable pairs, the analysis process terminates.
2. If a keypatch is interpreted in step 1, the control program enters into the scene phase. The production rules for the scene phase, which are described in the knowledge block SCENE, are activated to (re-)examine the keypatches which have not yet been interpreted. The agenda is updated.
3. The control program enters into the object phase corresponding to the object as which the patch(es) has just been interpreted in step 1. The production rules in the knowledge block of the object are activated to (re-)examine the patches touching the patch(es) just interpreted. The agenda is updated.
   GO TO 1.

This simple control scheme is an important outcome of the production system architecture; each production rule independently checks the database and modifies it whenever the condition is satisfied. However, two problems need to be considered to make this mechanism actually work: scheduling or focussing of attention (a method to direct the analysis to a goal) and conflict resolution (a method to resolve conflict among executable actions which are inconsistent with one another).

Conflict resolution   In a production system architecture, it is an important and difficult problem to resolve the conflicts between the modules (rules) which work concurrently and independently to modify the database. In our system, each production rule individually tries to assign a label to a patch whenever the patch satisfies the condition attached to the rule. It is usually the case that a patch simultaneously satisfies the conditions of several production rules whose associated actions try to assign different labels to the patch.

Since the basic operation which changes the database in our system is assignment of an object label to a patch, the detection of the inconsistent actions is quite straightforward. Our solution for the problem of conflict resolution is as follows.

(1) Actions which are determined to be executable are registered on the agenda as action-patch pairs. The agenda schedules the execution of the registered action-patch pairs by the scheduling method which will be explained shortly.

(2) Whenever a patch is interpreted by executing an action, every action-patch pair which is going to give a different interpretation to the patch is declared inconsistent and deleted from the agenda.

(3) Once a patch is given a label, it is not examined any more.

Scheduling   Every executable action-patch pair in our system is registered on the agenda with its score, and the pair which has the highest score is executed to actually change the database. Thus the score plays an important role in directing the analysis toward the goal. The score given to an executable action-patch pair is calculated as the sum of a base value and a premium value.

The base value is a constant given to each production rule. It plays a role in specifying the order of analysis. In the outdoor scene analyzer, the base value of each rule is determined so that the analysis basically proceeds according to the following order: (1) detection of objects in the scene, (2) determination of exact boundaries between objects and analysis of detailed structures of the objects, (3) analysis of occlusion.

The premium value depends on the degree of satisfaction of the condition part of the production rule when the action part was determined to be executable. It plays a role in guiding the analysis toward the correct interpretation. The fuzzy truth-value of the fuzzy predicate in the condition part and the correctness value of the label on the plan are often used as a premium value.

To sum up, the analysis proceeds toward the goal, guided by the premium values, following the strategy specified by the base values.

94

4.4.3. Description of production rules

Knowledge blocks and production rules   The model in our system is described as a network of knowledge blocks which define the objects, materials, and concepts in the world given as a task. Like the rules for plan generation, the production rules are arranged and stored in the network of knowledge blocks. The production rules are divided into subsets according to the role they play in the analysis process. Each subset is stored in a particular knowledge block corresponding to its role; for instance, the subset for the scene phase analysis is stored in the knowledge block SCENE, the subset to analyze the "sky" in the object phase is in the knowledge block SKY, and so on. This enables the agenda to pick up and activate only the appropriate and effective production rules according to the phases in the analysis process.

Format of production rules   The production rules in our system have the following format.

        [(ACT <fuzzy-predicate> (THEN <action-list>)) <var-list>]

The ACT indicates that the rule is a production rule. The <fuzzy-predicate> is the condition part of the production rule. It examines the database and produces a 0-to-1 fuzzy truth-value. Its syntax is the same as that of fuzzy predicates in the GEN- and STR-type rules used for plan generation.
        The (THEN <action-list>) is the action part of the production rule. The <action-list> is a set of actions for manipulating the database to build the scene description. Each action is described as a form in Lisp, i.e., a list composed of a function name and its arguments. The <action-list> of to-do rules includes a function for calculating the score to be associated to the action.
        The <var-list> is a list of external variables to be used in the fuzzy predicate and the actions. Before evaluating the fuzzy predicate, the control program binds these external variables to regions or patches to be examined by the rule. The number of variables in the <var-list> is 0, 1, or 2. The <var-list> in the to-do rules for the scene phase analysis has exactly one variable, and a keypatch is assigned to it. The <var-list> in the to-do rules for the object phase has two variables; the first variable is bound to a patch which has not yet been interpreted, the second one to a region belonging to the object corresponding to that phase. In the case of if-done rules, the variables,

if any, are bound to the same patch or region that is examined by the to-do rule which triggered the if-done rule.

Description of actions   Tne action part of a production rule includes a list of actions which manipulate the scene description. The manipulation is a combination of several simple operations.

(1) Patch-level operation
    A patch is assigned with a label --- (P-LABEL <label>).
(2) Region-level operation
    The patch is merged with a region --- (R-MERGE <region>).
    If the description of the region has not been created yet, a new region is created --- (R-CREATE).
(3) Object-level operation
    When a new region is created at the region-level operation, the region is associated with an object. A pointer representing a relation between the region and other regions belonging to that object is set --- (O-MERGE WITH <relation> <region>).
    If the description of the object has not been created yet, a new object is created and the region is associated with it --- (O-CREATE).
(4) Scene-level operation
    When a new description is created at the object-level operation, it is linked to the description of scene --- (S-MERGE).

When a patch is interpreted, one of the following three combinations of actions actually takes place.

    (a) P-LABEL & R-MERGE ,
    (b) P-LABEL & [R-CREATE] & O-MERGE ,
    (c) P-LABEL & [R-CREATE] & [O-CREATE] & [S-MERGE] .

The actions enclosed by [] are defaulted and tney are not explicitly described in the model. In the action-list of a production rule, these actions are described as the arguments of the functions which register them on the agenda. We use two functions for this purpose: CONCLUDE and MUST-BE. The function CONCLUDE registers the action, specified in its arguments, on the agenda with the patch given in the var-list. A score calculated by the SCORE-IS function in

96

the action-list is associated with the action. The function MUST-BE registers an action-patch pair which must be executed when the action registered by CONCLUDE in the same action-list is executed. The MUST-BE function allows defining an operation which manipulates a set of patches at a time (see the next section for an example).

Examples

Figure 4-9 shows a to-do rule to be used for the scene phase analysis. Its responsibility is to detect a keypatch corresponding to "sky", and to assemble it into the scene description. The fuzzy predicate in the condition part is a fuzzy logical-product of two predicates PROBABLY and NOTFOUND. The predicate PROBABLY refers to the plan and examines the correctness value of the label SKY for the keypatch which is assigned to the external variable *PCH. The predicate NOTFOUND produces 1.0 (i.e. true), if the description of the object SKY has not yet been included in the scene description.

The action-list of the rule contains two actions: labeling the patch, and creating the description of the object SKY. The function SCORE-IS calculates a score attached to the action to be registered on the agenda. The base value is 4.0 and the premium value is the degree of confidence of the label SKY for the keypatch *PCH.

Figure 4-10 illustrates another example. It is a to-do rule to be evaluated in the object phase to analyze an object "building". It has the responsibility of interpreting "windows", a substructure of the "building". In order to interprete the "windows", it is necessary to assign the label "window" to all the patches that are of rectangular shape and are arranged in a particular way within the area which has been interpreted as "building" (see figure 4-10-a).

```
[(ACT (AND (PROBABLY SKY *PCH)
           (NOTFOUND SKY))
      (THEN (CONCLUDE P-LABEL SKY)
            (CONCLUDE O-CREATE)
            (SCORE-IS (ADD 4.0 (CONFIDENCE-VALUE *PCH)))))
                                            (*PCH)]
```

Figure 4-9. A to-do rule for "sky" detection.

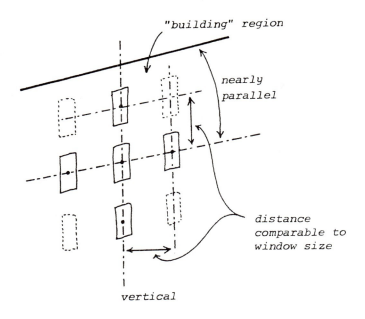

"building" region

nearly
parallel

distance
comparable to
window size

vertical

(a) "windows" and "building"

```
[(ACT (IF (AND (IS-PLAN *PCH *MRGN)                    · · · · · · · · · · (1)
                (*VERTICALLY-LONG *PCH))
           (THEN (GET-SET *PLSET (PLAN *MRGN) PATCHES)   · · · · · · · (2)
                 (AND (ALL-FETCH *WLIKE *PLSET           · · · · · · · · · · (3)
                        (AND (IS (LABEL *WLIKE) NIL)
                             (*VERTICALLY-LONG *WLIKE)))
                      (ALL-FETCH *WIND *WLIKE            · · · · · · · · · · (4)
                        (THERE-IS *WK *WLIKE
                           (*W-RELATION *WIND *WK))))))))
      (THEN (CONCLUDE P-LABEL B-WINDOW)
            (FOR-EACH *WIND (AND (MUST-BE *WIND P-LABEL B-WINDOW)
                                 (DONE-FOR *WIND)))
            (SCORE-IS (ADD 2.1 (DIV (NUMBER-OF *WIND) 100.0)))))
                                                  (*PCH *MRGN)]
```

(b) listing of the to-do rule for "windows" detection

Figure 4-10. A to-do rule for "windows" detection.

This operation is described by the rule in figure 4-10-b. The functions, GET-SET, ALL-FETCH, and THERE-IS, employed in the rule actively fetch a region (patch) or a set of regions (patches) from the database.

The control program binds a patch which is not yet interpreted to the external variable *PCH, and a region interpreted as a "building" to the external variable *MRGN. The fuzzy predicate in the condition part of the rule takes two roles: (1) It examines the status of the patch *PCH, and (2) it fetches a set of patches which match the condition specified in the predicate. The meaning of each part of the predicate is as follows:

(1) The predicate IS-PLAN checks whether the patch *PCH is included in the plan region of *MRGN. The predicate *VERTICALLY-LONG examines the crude shape of the patch *PCH.

(2) The function GET-SET fetches all the patches that are merged into the plan region corresponding to the region *MRGN. As the result, a set of patches which are included in the area around *MRGN is assigned to the variable *PLSET.

(3) The function ALL-FETCH fetches all the patches that have not yet been interpreted and whose shape satisfies the predicate *VERTICALLY-LONG. The patches are fetched out of the set *PLSET, and the selected patches are assigned to *WLIKE.

(4) The function ALL-FETCH fetches all the patches that have at least one partner patch within the set *WLIKE with which the relation *W-RELATION holds. The predicate *W-RELATION examines the placement relation which is illustrated in figure 4-10-a. A set of patches are fetched out of the patches in the set *WLIKE and assigned to the variable *WIND.

The action part includes the following actions. The function CONCLUDE registers a P-LABEL action on the agenda to assign the label B-WINDOW to the patch *PCH. The function MUST-BE also registers on the agenda the labeling operation to the patch in the set *WIND. Further operations to assemble them into the scene description are described by if-done rules in the knowledge-block B-WINDOW (see appendix B). The function SCORE-IS calculates the score for the action. The premium value is the number of patches which are extracted as the "window".

4.5. Experiments

4.5.1. Implementation

The analysis scheme described in the preceding sections was applied to obtain meaningful segmentations of outdoor scenes. Each scene is a shot on the campus of Kyoto University. Ordinary 35mm color transparency films were used to take the photographs. A color flying-spot-scanner was used to digitize the photographs. The digitization was performed with 256×256 size and 5-bit or 6-bit density resolution for each of the red, green, and blue components of color.

The systems for the preliminary segmentation and the rule-based analysis were implemented in FORTRAN which was augmented with specially designed functions for image manipulation and list processing.

The facilities for image manipulation enable users of the FORTRAN system to deal with the image arrays on disk files as if they were on the 2-D arrays defined in FORTRAN programs.

The facilities for list processing enable users to write programs in the same fashion as the "program feature" in Lisp. Pointers are manipulated as integer variables in FORTRAN. Elementary Lisp functions such as CONS, CAR, CDR, RPLACA, RPLACD, etc. and list I/O functions were implemented as FORTRAN functions. Moreover, our FORTRAN system allows recursion in function calling. Thus we could easily implement a system which needs to handle list structures such as the model and the scene description in the framework of FORTRAN.

The objects "sky", "building", "tree", and "road" were defined in the model. The "windows" of buildings were also defined as substructures of "building". The "car" and its "shadow" were defined as substructures of "road". "Concrete", "brick", "tile", "asphalt", and "leaves" were defined as materials of the "building", "road", and "tree". The number of rules described in each knowledge block is shown in Table 4-1. Table 4-2 presents the fuzzy predicates defined and used to describe the rules. The number of predicates for properties is 19, and that for relations is 15. Predicates which examine the plan and the scene description were also used. Table 4-3 shows the functions used to derive pictorial features from the image represented in the Patchery Data Structure. The table also includes the functions which were defined to retrieve information from the plan and the scene description. A complete listing of the model is included in appendix B.

100

Table 4-1.   Number of rules in each knowledge block.

	SCENE	SKY	TREE	BUILDING	ROAD	material*	total
property	-	5	2	4	3	6	20
relation	-	2	0	2	3	0	7
production (to-do)	8	3	2	4	4	-	21
(if-done)	2	1	1	5	0	-	9
total	10	11	5	15	10	6	57

*material: CONCRETE, TILE, etc. (cf. Fig. 4-5)

Table 4-2.   Fuzzy predicates used to describe the model.

property	color	*DARK, *BRIGHT, *SHINING, *GREY, *VIVID, *RED, *BLUE, *GREEN, *YELLOW	9
	position	*UPPER, *MIDDLE, *LOWER	3
	shape	*HORIZONTALLY-LONG, *VERTICALLY-LONG *MANYHOLE, *MANYLINE, *HOLELINE	5
	texture	*TEXTURAL, *HEAVY-TEXTURE	2
relation	color	*SAME-COLOR, *LOW-CONTRAST, *DARKER	3
	position	*WITH-IN, *CONTACT, TOUCHING, FACING (HORIZONTALLY, VERTICALLY), POSITION (UP, DOWN), ABOVE, BELOW, BETWEEN, *W-RELATION, SAME-ZONE, DIFFERENT-ZONE	11
	shape	*LINEAR-BOUNDARY	1
description		PROBABLY, MAY-BE, NOTFOUND, IS, IS-PLAN	5

101

Table 4-3. Functions being used to describe the model.

property	color	INTENSITY, SATURATION, HUE, RED-VALUE, GREEN-VALUE, BLUE-VALUE, CONTOUR-CONTRAST	7
	position	MASS-CENTER-X, MASS-CENTER-Y, V-ZONE, MBR-UP-SIDE, MBR-LOW-SIDE, MBR-LEFT-SIDE, MBR-RIGHT-SIDE	7
	shape	AREA, CONTOUR-LENGTH, VH-RATIO, COMPACTNESS, WIDTH-X, WIDTH-Y, HOLE-NUMBER, LINE-DEGREE, HOLE-LINE-DEGREE	9
	texture	TEXTURE-DEGREE	1
relation	color	R-G-B-DIFFERENCE, CHROMATIC-DIFFERENCE, BOUNDARY-CONTRAST	3
	position	DISTANCE, ANGLE-DIFFERENCE, O-RATIO	3
	shape	BOUNDARY-LENGTH, BOUNDARY-LINE-DEGREE, T-RATIO	3
description		ALL-FETCH, THERE-IS, T-FETCH, GET-SET, OF, LABEL, REGION, OBJECT, PLAN, MASTER, ASK-VALUE, CONFIDENCE-VALUE	12

4.5.2. Results

Figure 4-11-a is a digitized input scene. Figure 4-11-b shows the result of preliminary segmentation. The patches with area greater than 300 were selected as keypatches. Figure 4-11-c is the plan image. Figure 4-12 illustrates the plans generated during the analysis of the scene. The brightness of each region indicates the degree of correctness of the labels, SKY, TREE, BUILDING, and ROAD, for that region in the plan image. Figure 4-12-a is the plan evaluated using only the property rules. Notice that the region corresponding to this side of the building was accidentally assigned a high correctness value for SKY because its color is grey and very bright. Figure 4-12-b shows the plan revised by using the relation rules. The same region now obtains a high correctness value for BUILDING by means of the rules which represent the relation between the "building" and the "sky". Figure 4-12-c is the plan revised after the scene horizon was detected by a production rule. The position of the extracted horizon is indicated in the figure. The rule to detect the scene horizon was implemented as an if-done rule in the knowledge-block SCENE. It is activated when the plan is modified and searches for enough evidence of the position of horizon. Roughly speaking, the position is defined by using the outstanding horizontal boundaries between the "probably-road" and the "probably-non-road" regions in the plan image. The actual definition of the rule can be found in appendix B.

Figure 4-12-d illustrates the outlines of the "building" extracted by an if-done rule which was activated when the object "building" is created. Figure 4-11-d is the final result of segmentation. It plots the contours of the regions and sub-regions in the scene description created through the analysis. The "windows" of the building are successfully analyzed. Note that the images in figures 4-11-b, c, d, and 4-12 are generated only for visualization. In our region analyzer all data included in those images are recorded symbolically in the database.

Figure 4-13 shows another example. The scene in figure 4-13-a includes a car on a road. Figure 4-13-b is the result of preliminary segmentation. Figure 4-13-c shows the plan image and figure 4-13-d shows the segmentation finally obtained. The car and its shadow were successfully analyzed. Figure 4-14 illustrates the plans generated for the scene in figure 4-13.

Figures 4-15 and 4-16 show the result for another scene which also includes a car on the road.

(a) digitized input scene

(b) result of preliminary
segmentation

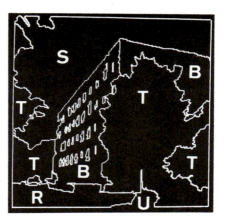

(c) plan image

(d) result of meaningful
segmentation
S: sky, T: tree, R: road,
B: building, U: unknown.

Figure 4-11. Result of the rule-based analysis: Example 1.
(See color section opposite page 72 for color reproduction of (a).)

(a) first plan obtained by
    using only the property
    rules

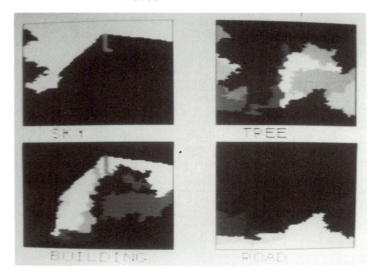

(b) after using the relation
    rules

Figure 4-12. Plans generated for the scene of Fig. 4-11.

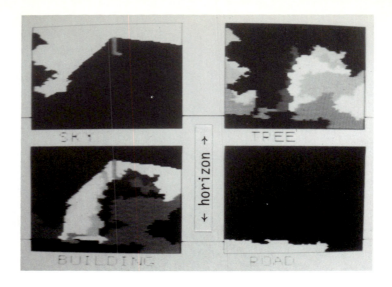

(c) after extracting the horizon
by the top-down analysis

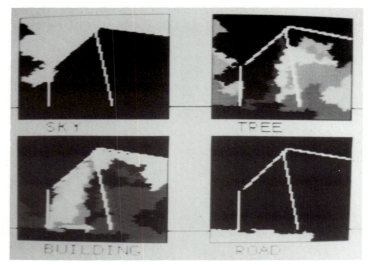

(d) outlines of the building
extracted by the top-down
analysis

Figure 4-12. (continued.)

106

(a) digitized input scene

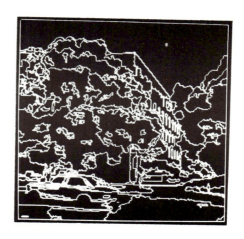

(b) result of preliminary
segmentation

(c) plan image

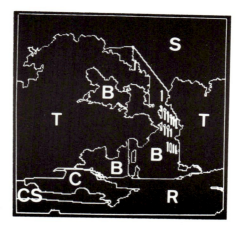

(d) result of meaningful
segmentation
S: sky, T: tree, B: building,
R: road, C: car,
CS: car shadow.

Figure 4-13.   Result of the rule-based analysis: Example 2.
(See color section opposite page 72 for color reproduction of (a).)

(a) first plan obtained by
    using only the property
    rules

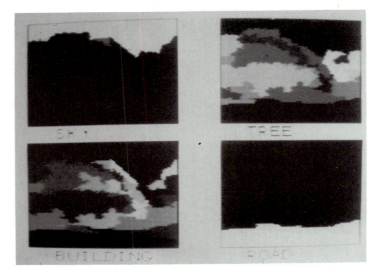

(b) after using the relation
    rules

Figure 4-14. Plans generated for the scene of Fig. 4-13.

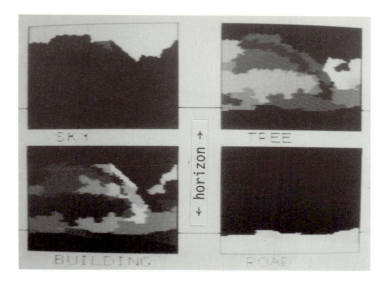

(c) after extracting the horizon
by the top-down analysis

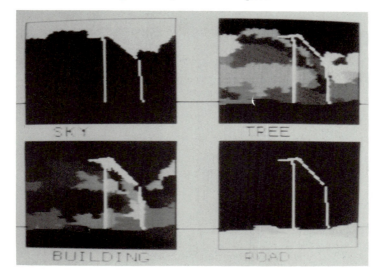

(d) outlines of the building
extracted by the top-down
analysis

Figure 4-14. (continued.)

(a) digitized input scene

(b) result of preliminary
segmentation

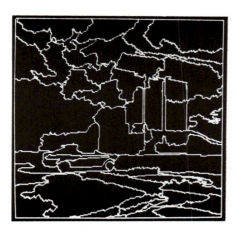

(c) plan image

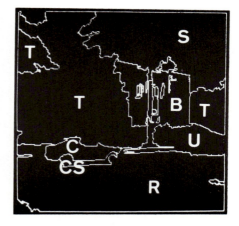

(d) result of meaningful
segmentation
S: sky, T: tree, B: building,
R: road, C: car, U: unknown,
CS: car shadow.

Figure 4-15.   Result of the rule-based analysis: Example 3.

(See color section opposite page 72 for color reproduction of (a).)

(a) first plan obtained by
    using only the property
    rules

(b) after using the relation
    rules

Figure 4-16. Plans generated for the scene of Fig. 4-15.

111

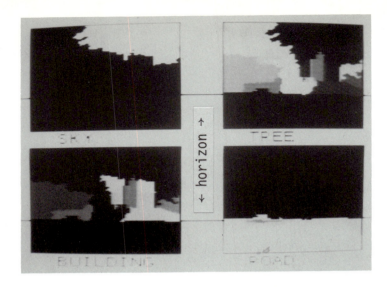

(c) after extracting the horizon
by the top-down analysis

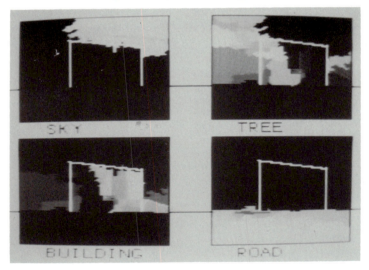

(d) outlines of the building
extracted by the top-down
analysis

Figure 4-16. (continued.)

4.6. Conclusion

In this chapter, we described a rule-based region analyzer which can deal with rather complex scenes including objects with substructures. Outdoor scenes from our university campus were analyzed by the system.

The following results have been achieved.

(1) A top-down control scheme was applied to the region growing method. This enables the region analysis to deal with the detailed structures in the scene, such as the windows of a building, which has been difficult for the so-called semantic region analysis.

(2) A plan of the input scene is generated by the bottom-up control scheme. It is effectively combined with the top-down analysis implemented by using the production system architecture. As a result, a data-driven control mechanism can be realized to improve reliability of the analysis; the portions of the scene which can be analyzed with high confidence are analyzed before other portions with low confidence.

(3) We have developed a scheme for approximate reasoning to handle the four kinds of uncertainty existing in (a) pictorial features, (b) property definitions, (c) object descriptions, and (d) interpretation results. Fuzzy predicates are used for the uncertainty in (a) and (b). The fuzzy truth-values and the uncertainty in (c) and (d) are incorporated into the computation of the revision factors used for plan evaluation.

(4) The region growing process has a clear control structure: selecting a region (patch) which has not been interpreted yet, assigning an object label to it, and assembling it into the scene description. By applying this structure together with the basic control scheme of the production system architecture, we have achieved a simple and clear knowledge representation scheme for image analysis.

(5) A production system architecture was utilized in image analysis. Several problems were addressed and solved concerning the modeling, computation, scheduling, etc. Especially, in order to reduce the computation, two phases (scene phase and object phase) were established in the control structure based on two opposite properties (globality and locality) of the scene.

5 Conclusion

A region analysis system for natural color scenes has been intensively studied. In the system described here, the input image is converted once into a structured data network, and the knowledge to be used in the higher-level analysis is coded as a set of rules which work on this network.

A wide range of issues have been dealt with in this paper from signal domains to semantic ones.

Color Information   In chapter 2, we discussed the use of color information in region segmentation. Systematic experiments were performed to examine the role of color information. A segmentation scheme, called the "dynamic K-L transformation", was developed for this purpose. We have found a set of color features that can approximate all the color features used in segmenting various color images by the dynamic K-L transformation. The effectiveness of the color features was verified by a comparative study with various sets of color features from the view point of segmentation and computation. An experiment showing that the color in natural scenes is physically almost two-dimensional was also presented in this chapter.

Signal-level segmentation   In chapter 3, we presented a system for preliminary segmentation. A powerful segmentation program was developed, based on an algorithm which uses multihistograms to find the cutoff values for partitioning. Schemes were developed to improve the quality of segmentation, including a scheme for avoiding the fragmentation of textural parts and a scheme for extracting the detailed structures veiled by dominant ones.

Symbolic data structure for segmented images   The result of segmentation is organized into a well-structured symbolic data network with powerful retrieval facilities. It includes the properties and relations of regions and supports the merging operation of regions. Only the "primary" features are described in the network. The "secondary" features can be derived easily from the primary ones when they become to be necessary. The system has been applied to various color images.

Rule-based region analysis for interpretation Chapter 4 described a rule-based region analyzer. Bottom-up control and top-down control were effectively combined in the framework of region growing. The system generates a plan via bottom-up control as a representation of the rough structures in the input scene. A scheme of approximate reasoning was developed to handle the uncertainty contained in the knowledge and the pictorial data.

A symbolic description of the input scene is made via top-down analysis. The top-down process was constructed using a production system architecture. Employing region growing as the basic control structure of the production system, we have achieved a simple and clear knowledge representation scheme for image analysis. In order to reduce the computation needed to manage the production system, two phases (scene phase and object phase) have been successfully established in the control structure utilizing the two opposite properties (globality and locality) of scenes.

Successful analysis of outdoor scenes including sky, trees, buildings, and roads have been demonstrated.

References

Bajcsy,R. and Lieberman,L.I.
"Computer Description of Real Outdoor Scenes",
Proc. IJCPR-II(1974) pp.174-179.

Barrow,H.G. and Popplestone,R.J.
"Relational Descriptions in Picture Processing",
Machine Intelligence, Vol.6, (Meltzer,B. and Michie,D., eds.),
American Elsevier, New York(1971), pp.377-396.

Brice,C. and Fennema,C.
"Scene Analysis Using Regions",
Artificial Intelligence, Vol.1(1971), pp.205-226.

Davis,R. and King,J.
"An Overview of Production System",
AIM-271(1975), Stanford University.

Duda,R.O. and Hart,P.E.
"Pattern Classification and Scene Analysis",
p.338, John Wiley and Sons, New York(1973).

Freuder,E.C.
"A Computer System for Visual Recognition Using Active
Knowledge",
Proc. IJCAI-V(1977), pp.671-677.

Hewitt,C.
"PLANNER",
A.I.Memo 168(1966), A.I. Lab. MIT.

Horowitz,S. and Pavlidis,T.
"Picture Segmentation by a Directed Split-and-Merge Procedure",
Proc. IJCPR-II(1974), pp.424-433.

Kanade,T.
"Computer Recognition of Human Faces",
ISR-47, Birkhauser(1977).

Kanade,T.

         "Region Segmentation: Signal vs. Semantics",
         Proc. IJCPR-IV(1978), pp.95-105.

Kender,J.R.

         "Saturation, Hue, and Normalized Color; Calculation,
         Digitization Effects, and Use",
         Technical Report, Department of Computer Science, Carnegie-
         Mellon University(1976).

Kunii,T. Weyl,S. and Tenenbaum,J.

         "A Relational Data Base Schema for Describing Complex Pictures
         with Color and Texture",
         Information Processing '74(1974), pp.310-316.

Lee,C.T. and Chang,C.L.

         "Some Properties of Fuzzy Logic",
         Information and Control, Vol.19, No.5(1971), pp.417-431.

Marr,D.

         "Early Processing of Visual Information",
         A.I.Memo 340(1975), A.I. Lab. MIT.

Nevatia, R.

         "A Color Edge Detector",
         Proc. IJCPR-III(1976), pp.829-832.

Ohlander,R.

         "Analysis of Natural Scenes",
         Ph.D. Thesis, Department of Computer Science, Carnegie-Mellon
         University(1975).

Pavlidis,T.

         "Segmentation by Texture Using a Co-Occurrence Matrix and
         a Split-and-Merge Algorithm",
         Computer Graphics and Image Processing, Vol.10, No.2
         (1979), pp.172-182.

Pratt,W.K.

         "Digital Image Processing",
         p.78, John Wiley & Sons, New York(1978).

Preparata,F.P. and Ray,S.R.

         "An Approach to Artificial Non-Symbolic Cognition",
         Information Science, Vol.4(1972), pp.65-86.

Riseman,E. et al.

        "I. Segmentation Processes in the VISIONS System",

        "II. Model-Building in the VISIONS System",

        "III. Between Regions and Objects -- Surfaces and Volumes",

        Proc. IJCAI-V(1977), pp.642-647.

Rubin,S.M. and Reddy,R.

        "The Locus Model of Search and its Use in Image Interpretation",

        Proc. IJCAI-V(1977), pp.590-595.

Sakai,T. Nagao,M. and Kanade,T.

        "Computer Analysis and Classification of Photographs of Human

        Faces",

        Proc. First USA-JAPAN Computer Conference(1972), pp.55-62.

Shortliffe, E. H.

        "Computer-based Medical Consultations: MYCIN".

        American Elsevier, New York(1976).

Sloan,K.R.

        "World Model Driven Recognition of Natural Scenes",

        Ph.D. Thesis, The Moore School of Electrical Engineering,

        University of Pennsylvania(1977).

Tanimoto,S. and Pavlidis,T.

        "A Hierarchical Data Structure for Picture Processing",

        Computer Graphics and Image Processing, Vol.4, No.2(1975), pp.104-

        119.

Tenenbaum,J.M. and Barrow,H.G.

        "Experiments in Interpretation-Guided Segmentation",

        Artificial Intelligence, Vol.8(1976), pp.241-274.

Tomita,F. Yachida,M. and Tsuji,S.

        "Detection of Homogeneous Regions by Structural Analysis",

        Proc. IJCAI-III(1973), pp.564-571.

Waltz, D.

        "Understanding Line Drawings of Scenes with Shadows"'

        in The Psychology of Computer Vision, P.H.Winston ed.,

        McGraw-Hill, New York(1975).

Yakimovsky,Y. and Feldman,J.A.

        "A Semantics-Based Decision Theory Region Analyzer",

        Proc. IJCAI-III(1973), pp.580-588.

Appendix-A Supplementary Results of Preliminary Segmentation

(a) digitized image

(b) result of segmentation

(c) straight line segments

(d) reconstructed image

417 regions, 1156 boundary segments, 763 vertices,
477 line segments, 25 holes.

Figure A-1.

(a) digitized image   (b) result of segmentation

(c) straight line segments   (d) reconstructed image

415 regions, 1174 boundary segments, 773 vertices,
328 line segments, 15 holes.

Figure A-2.

(a) digitized image

(b) result of segmentation

(c) straight line segments

(d) reconstructed image

487 regions, 1374 boundary segments, 908 vertices,
504 line segments, 21 holes.

Figure A-3.

Appendix-B Complete Listing of the Model

```
*SCENE   knowledge-block-of-scene

(OBJECTS (*SKY *TREE *BUILDING *ROAD *UNKNOWN)
SUB-OBJECTS (*B-WINDOW *CAR *C-SHADOW)
KEY-PATCH-IS [(GREATERP (AREA *PCH) 300)(*PCH)]

PLAN-IMAGE-GENERATION [(DIV (BOUNDARY-LENGTH *PCH *KPCH)
                            (MULT (R-G-B-DIFFERENCE *PCH *KPCH)
                                  (BOUNDARY-CONTRAST *PCH *KPCH)))
                                              (*PCH *KPCH)]


IF-PLAN-IS-MODIFIED (IF-DONE (

rule-for-horizon-detection
[(ACT (IF (IS (OF HORIZON (SCENE))) NIL)
          (ALL-FETCH *HRGN *PLAN-REGIONS
           (IF (AND (NOT (PROBABLY ROAD *HRGN))
                    (NOT (TOUCHING *HRGN LOW-SIDE))
                    (ALL-FETCH *WRGN *PLAN-REGIONS
                     (IF (AND (MAY-BE ROAD *WRGN)
                              (ABOVE *HRGN *WRGN)
                              (NOT (*SAME-COLOR *HRGN *WRGN))
                              (FACING HORIZONTALLY *HRGN *WRGN))
                           (MULT (SUB (FACING HORIZONTALLY *HRGN *WRGN) 0.5)
                                 (SUB (MIN (ASK-VALUE ROAD *WRGN) 0.6)
                                      (ASK-VALUE ROAD *HRGN) )))))
                 (VALUE *WRGN *WRGN) )))
        (THEN (MEMO (SCENE) ROAD-ZONE
                           (WITH (MBR-LOW-SIDE *HRGN) 256 1 256))
              (MEMO (SCENE) HORIZON (MBR-LOW-SIDE *HRGN))
              (EXECUTE PLAN-EVALUATION) )) ] ))


P-SELECT (TO-DO (

rule-for-initial-start
[(ACT (AND (PROBABLY BUILDING *PCH) (NOTFOUND BUILDING))
```

```
        (THEN (CONCLUDE P-LABEL BUINDING)
              (SCORE-IS (ADD 4.0 (CONFIDENCE-VALUE *PCH))))))(*PCH)]
[(ACT (AND (PROBABLY ROAD *PCH)(NOTFOUND ROAD))
        (THEN (CONCLUDE P-LABEL ROAD)
              (SCORE-IS (ADD 4.0 (CONFIDENCE-VALUE *PCH))))))(*PCH)]
[(ACT (AND (PROBABLY SKY *PCH)(NOTFOUND SKY))
        (THEN (CONCLUDE P-LABEL SKY)
              (SCORE-IS (ADD 4.0 (CONFIDENCE-VALUE *PCH))))))(*PCH)]
[(ACT (AND (PROBABLY TREE *PCH)
          (NOT (THERE-IS *TR *REGIONS
                  (AND (IS (LABEL *TR) TREE)
                       (OR (TOUCHING (PLAN *PCH)(PLAN *TR))
                           (*WITH-IN2 (PLAN *PCH)
                                       (V-ZONE2 30 (PLAN *TR))))))))
        (THEN (CONCLUDE P-LABEL TREE)
              (SCORE-IS (ADD 4.0 (CONFIDENCE-VALUE *PCH))))))(*PCH)]


rule-for-adjacent-wall-of-building
[(ACT (AND (MAY-BE BUILDING *PCH)
          (THERE-IS *BL *REGIONS
            (AND (IS (LABEL *BL) BUILDING)
                 (NOT (IS (OF SHAPE VIEW (OBJECT *BL)) 1))
                 (IS (OF ADJACENT (OBJECT *BL)) NIL)
                 (DIFFERNT-ZONE *PCH *BL))))
        (THEN (CONCLUDE P-LABEL BUILDING)
              (CONCLUDE O-MERGE (WITH ADJACENT *BL))
              (SCORE-IS (ADD 5.0 (ASK-VALUE BUILDING *PCH)))))(*PCH)]


rule-for-building-occlusion
[(ACT (AND (MAY-BE BUILDING *PCH)
          (THERE-IS *BL *REGIONS
            (AND (IS (LABEL *BL) BUILDING)
                 (SAME-ZONE *PCH *BL)
                 (*SAME-COLOR *PCH *BL)
                 (THERE-IS *TR *KEYPATCHES
                   (AND (BETWEEN *TR *PCH *BL)
                        (OR (IS (LABEL *TR) TREE)
                            (AND (IS (LABEL *TR) BUILDING)
                                 (NOT (IS (OBJECT *BL)
                                          (OBJECT *TR)))))))))))
        (THEN (CONCLUDE P-LABEL BUILDING)
              (CONCLUDE O-MERGE (WITH OCCLUDE *BL (REGION *TR)))
              (SCORE-IS (ADD 1.0 (ASK-VALUE BUILDING *PCH)))))(*PCH)]
```

```
   rule-for-tree-occlusion
[(ACT (AND (*DARK *PCH)(*UPPER *PCH)
            (OR (TOUCHING *PCH UP-SIDE)(TOUCHING *PCH SIDE))
            (THERE-IS *TR *REGIONS
             (AND (IS (LABEL *TR) TREE)
                  (ABOVE *PCH *TR)
                  (TOUCHING *TR SIDE)
                  (*WITH-IN2 *PCH (V-ZONE *TR)))))
       (THEN (CONCLUDE P-LABEL TREE)
             (CONCLUDE O-MERGE (WITH OCCLUDE *TR FRAME))
             (SCORE-IS 1.0)))(*PCH)]

   rule-for-tree-garbage
[(ACT (PROBABLY TREE *PCH)
       (THEN (CONCLUDE P-LABEL TREE)
             (SCORE-IS (ASK-VALUE TREE *PCH))))(*PCH)]   ))


P-LABEL (IF-DONE (

if-done-rule-to-be-activated-when-keypatch-is-labeled
[(ACT (NOT (IS (OF PLAN *PCH) NIL))
       (THEN (EXECUTE PLAN-EVALUATION)))(*PCH)]   ))   )



*SKY   knowledge-block-of-sky

(PROPERTY-RULES (
 [(GEN (NOT (*LOWER *RGN))(1.0 . 0.6))(*RGN)]
 [(GEN (*SHINING *RGN)(1.0 . 0.2))(*RGN)]
 [(GEN (OR (*BLUE *RGN)(*GREY *RGN))(1.0 . 0.2))(*RGN)]
 [(GEN (NOT (*TEXTURAL *RGN))(1.0 . 0.7))(*RGN)]
 [(STR (TOUCHING *RGN UP-SIDE)(0.7 . 0.2))(*RGN)] )

 RELATION-RULES (
 [(STR (AND (*LINEAR-BOUNDARY *RGN *RGN2)
            (IF *LINEAR-BOUNDARY (POSITION DOWN *RGN *RGN2)))
                        (0.0 . 0.5) FOR SKY)(*RGN *RGN2)]
 [(STR (IF (NOT (IS (OF BUILDING-ZONE (SCENE)) NIL))
           (FUZZY1 (O-RATIO *RGN (OF BUILDING-ZONE (SCENE))) 0.5 0.9))
                        (0.0 . 0.5) FOR SCENE)(*RGN)])
```

```
P-SELECT (

TO-DO (
[(ACT (MAY-BE SKY *PCH)
      (THEN (SCORE-IS (ADD 2.0 (ASK-VALUE SKY *PCH)))))(*PCH)]
[(ACT (AND (IS-PLAN *PCH *MRGN)(*BRIGHT *PCH))
      (THEN (SCORE-IS 3.0)))(*PCH *MRGN)]
[(ACT (*BRIGHT *PCH)(THEN (SCORE-IS 0.05)))(*PCH)]  )

IF-DONE (
[(ACT *T* (THEN (CONCLUDE P-LABEL SKY)
                (CONCLUDE R-MERGE (MASTER *PCH))))(*PCH)] ))

APRIORI-VALUE-IS 0.1)




*TREE   knowledge-block-of-tree

(MADE-OF (*LEAVES)

 PROPERTY-RULES (
 [(GEN (*MIDDLE *RGN)(0.6 . 0.3))(*RGN)]
 [(STR (*HEAVY-TEXTURE *RGN)(0.8 . 0.2))(*RGN)]  )

 P-SELECT (

 TO-DO (
 [(ACT (MAY-BE TREE *PCH)
       (THEN (SCORE-IS (ADD 2.0 (ASK-VALUE TREE *PCH)))))(*PCH)]
 [(ACT (AND (IS-PLAN *PCH *MRGN)(NOT (*SHINING *PCH)))
       (THEN (SCORE-IS 3.0)))(*PCH *MRGN)]

 IF-DONE (
 [(ACT *T* (THEN (CONCLUDE P-LABEL TREE)
                 (CONCLUDE R-MERGE (MASTER *PCH))))(*PCH)] ))

 APRIORI-VALUE-IS 0.2)
```

```
*BUILDING  knowledge-block-of-building


(MADE-OF (OR *CONCRETE *TILE *BRICK)
 SUB-OBJECTS (*B-WINDOW)


 PROPERTY-RULES (
 [(GEN (*MIDDLE *RGN)(0.6 . 0.3))(*RGN)]
 [(STR (*MANYHOLE *RGN)(0.8 . 0.2))(*RGN)]
 [(STR (*MANYLINE *RGN)(0.4 . 0.2))(*RGN)]
 [(GEN (*HOLELINE *RGN)(0.9 . 0.5))(*RGN)]  )


 RELATION-RULES (
 [(GEN (AND (*LINEAR-BOUNDARY *RGN *RGN2)
            (IF *LINEAR-BOUNDARY (NOT (POSITION UP *RGN *RGN2))))
                              (0.8 . 0.4) FOR SKY)(*RGN *RGN2)]
 [(STR (IF (NOT (IS (OF BUILDING-ZONE (SCENE)) NIL))
           (AND (O-RATIO *RGN (OF BUILDING-ZONE (SCENE)))
                (*MANYLINE *RGN)))
               (0.9 . 0.3) FOR SCENE)(*RGN)]  )


 P-SELECT (


 TO-DO (
 [(ACT (AND (MAY-BE BUILDING *PCH)(SAME-ZONE *PCH *MRGN))
       (THEN (CONCLUDE P-LABEL BUILDING)
             (CONCLUDE R-MERGE *MRGN)
             (SCORE-IS (ADD 2.0 (ASK-VALUE BUILDING *PCH)))))
                                           (*PCH *MRGN)]
 [(ACT (AND (NOT (IS-PLAN *PCH *MRGN))(SAME-ZONE *PCH *MRGN)
            (MAY-BE BUILDING (PLAN *PCH)))
       (THEN (CONCLUDE P-LABEL BUILDING)
             (CONCLUDE R-MERGE *MRGN)
             (SCORE-IS (ADD 1.95 (ASK-VALUE BUILDING (PLAN *PCH))))))
                                           (*PCH *MRGN)]


 rule-for-window-extraction
 [(ACT (IF (AND (IS-PLAN *PCH *MRGN)(SAME-ZONE *PCH *MRGN)
                (*VERTICALLY-LONG *PCH)(*CONTACT *PCH (PLAN *MRGN)))
           (THEN (GET-SET *PLSET (PLAN *MRGN) PATCHES)
                 (AND (ALL-FETCH *WLIKE *PLSET
                      (AND (IS (LABEL *WLIKE) NIL)
                           (SAME-ZONE *WLIKE *MRGN)
                           (*VERTICALLY-LONG *WLIKE)
                           (*CONTACT *WLIKE (PLAN *MRGN))))
```

128

```
                      (THERE-IS *WK *WLIKE (*W-RELATION *PCH *WK))
                      (ALL-FETCH *WIND *WLIKE
                       (THERE-IS *WK *WLIKE
                        (*W-RELATION *WIND *WK))))))
       (THEN (CONCLUDE P-LABEL B-WINDOW)
             (FOR-EACH *WIND (AND (MUST-BE *WIND P-LABEL B-WINDOW)
                                  (DONE-FOR *WIND)))
             (SCORE-IS (ADD 2.1 (DIV (NUMBER-OF *WIND) 100.0)))))
                                                     (*PCH *MRGN)]
 [(ACT (AND (IS-PLAN *PCH *MRGN)(SAME-ZONE *PCH *MRGN))
       (THEN (CONCLUDE P-LABEL BUILDING)
             (CONCLUDE R-MERGE *MRGN)
             (SCORE-IS 2.0)))(*PCH *MRGN)]


O-MERGE (IF-DONE (
 [(ACT *T* (DESCRIBE-BUILDING (REGION *PCH)))(*PCH)] ))


O-CREATE (IF-DONE (
 [(ACT *T* (THEN (EXTRACT-BUILDING-SHAPE (REGION *PCH))
                 (DESCRIBE-BUILDING (REGION *PCH))
                 (EXECUTE PLAN-EVALUATION)))(*PCH)] ))


APRIORI-VALUE-IS 0.2)




*ROAD  knowledge-block-of-road

(MADE-OF (OR *ASPHALT *CONCRETE)
 SUB-OBJECTS (*CAR *C-SHADOW)

 PROPERTY-RULES (
 [(GEN (*LOWER *RGN)(0.8 . 0.4))(*RGN)]
 [(GEN (*HORIZONTALLY-LONG *RGN)(0.7 . 0.2))(*RGN)]
 [(STR (TOUCHING *RGN LOWER-SIDE)(0.9 . 0.2))(*RGN)] )

 RELATION-RULES (
 [(STR (AND (*SAME-COLOR *RGN *RGN2)(TOUCHING *RGN *RGN2))
                           (0.9 . 0.2) FOR ROAD)(*RGN *RGN2)]
 [(GEN (IF (NOT (IS (OF HORIZON (SCENE)) NIL))
           (O-RATIO *RGN (OF ROAD-ZONE (SCENE))))
                           (1.0 . 0.3) FOR SCENE)(*RGN)]
```

```
[(STR (IF (NOT (IS (OF HORIZON (SCENE)) NIL))
         (NOT (GREATERP (ADD (MBR-UP-SIDE *RGN) 10)
                        (OF HORIZON (SCENE))))))
                              (0.0 . 0.5) FOR SCENE) (*RGN)])


P-SELECT (

TO-DO (
[(ACT (IF (PROBABLY ROAD *PCH)
         (THEN (AND (*LOW-CONTRAST (PLAN *PCH) (PLAN *MRGN))
                    (NOT (OR (ABOVE *PCH *MRGN)
                             (BELOW *PCH *MRGN)))))))
     (THEN (CONCLUDE P-LABEL ROAD)
           (CONCLUDE R-MERGE *MRGN)
           (SCORE-IS (ADD *PREDICATE-VALUE 2.9)))) (*PCH *MRGN)]


rule-for-car-extraction
[(ACT (IF (MAY-BE ROAD *PCH)
         (THEN (AND (*HORIZONTALLY-LONG *PCH)
                    (*DARK *PCH)
                    (*DARKER *PCH *MRGN)
                    (POSITION UP (PLAN *PCH) (PLAN *MRGN))
                    (THERE-IS *CLIKE *KEYPATCHES
                     (AND (IS (LABEL *CLIKE) NIL)
                          (NOT (IS *CLIKE *PCH))
                          (*HORIZONTALLY-LONG (PLAN *CLIKE))
                          (*WITH-IN (PLAN *CLIKE)
                                    (V-ZONE (PLAN *PCH)))
                          (POSITION UP (PLAN *CLIKE)
                                       (PLAN *PCH)))) )))
     (THEN (ALL-FETCH *WK *KEYPATCHES
             (AND (IS (LABEL *WK) NIL)
                  (NOT (IS *WK *PCH))
                  (*HORIZONTALLY-LONG (PLAN *WK))
                  (*CONTACT2 (PLAN *WK) (PLAN *CLIKE))
                  (*LINEAR-BOUNDARY (PLAN *WK) (PLAN *CLIKE))
                  (*SAME-COLOR *WK *CLIKE)
                  (*WITH-IN (PLAN *WK) (V-ZONE (PLAN *PCH)))))
           (CONCLUDE P-LABEL C-SHADOW)
           (GET-SET *PLSET (PLAN *PCH) PATCHES)
           (FOR-EACH *PLSET
             (IF (NOT (IS *PLSET *PCH))
                 (THEN (MUST-BE *PLSET P-LABEL C-SHADOW)
                       (MUST-BE *PLSET R-MERGE *PCH)
                       (DONE-FOR *PLSET))))
```

130

```
                    (GET-SET *PLSET (PLAN *CLIKE) PATCHES)
                    (FOR-EACH *PLSET
                     (AND (MUST-BE *PLSET P-LABEL CAR)
                          (MUST-BE *PLSET R-MERGE *CLIKE)
                          (DONE-FOR *PLSET)))
                    (FOR-EACH *WK
                     (AND (GET-SET *PLSET (PLAN *WK) PATCHES)
                          (FOR-EACH *PLSET
                           (AND (MUST-BE *PLSET P-LABEL CAR)
                                (MUST-BE *PLSET R-MERGE *CLIKE)
                                (DONE-FOR *PLSET)))))
                    (SCORE-IS 2.95)))(*PCH *MRGN)]
[(ACT (MAY-BE ROAD *PCH)
      (THEN (CONCLUDE P-LABEL ROAD)
            (CONCLUDE R-MERGE *MRGN)
            (SCORE-IS (ADD 2.0 (ASK-VALUE ROAD *PCH)))))(*PCH *MRGN)]
[(ACT (AND (IS-PLAN *PCH *MRGN)
           (OR (*DARK *PCH)(*GREY *PCH)))
      (THEN (CONCLUDE P-LABEL ROAD)
            (CONCLUDE R-MERGE *MRGN)
            (SCORE-IS 3.0)))(*PCH *MRGN)] ))


APRIORI-VALUE-IS 0.1)



*UNKNOWN          knowledge-block-for-unknown-object

(APRIORI-VALUE-IS 0.1)



*B-WINDOW         knowledge-block-of-windows-of-building

(P-LABEL (IF-DONE (
  [(ACT (AND (T-FETCH *WK *PCH)
             (THERE-IS *WIND *WK (IS (LABEL *WIND) B-WINDOW)))
        (THEN (CONCLUDE R-MERGE *WIND)))(*PCH)] )))




*CONCRETE
(PROPERTY-RULES (
  [(GEN (AND (*BRIGHT *RGN)(*GREY *RGN))(0.6 . 0.2))(*RGN)] ))
```

```
*ASPHALT
(PROPERTY-RULES (
  [(GEN (AND (*DARK *RGN)(*GREY *RGN))(0.6 . 0.2))(*RGN)] ))



*TILE
(PROPERTY-RULES (
  [(GEN (AND (*YELLOW *RGN)(NOT (*VIVID *RGN)))(0.6 . 0.2))(*RGN)] ))



*BRICK
(PROPERTY-RULES (
  [(GEN (*RED *RGN)(0.6 . 0.1))(*RGN)] ))



*LEAVES
(PROPERTY-RULES (
  [(GEN (OR (*GREEN *RGN)(*YELLOW *RGN))(0.9 . 0.4))(*RGN)]
  [(GEN (*TEXTURAL *RGN)(0.7 . 0.4))(*RGN)] ))




*UPPER
(PROPERTY-DEFINITION ((*X)(FUZZY2 (MASS-CENTER-X *X) 50 150)))

*MIDDLE
(PROPERTY-DEFINITION ((*X)(FUZZY3 (MASS-CENTER-X *X) 0 100 150 250)))

*LOWER
(PROPERTY-DEFINITION ((*X)(FUZZY1 (MASS-CENTER-X *X) 150 220)))

*DARK
(PROPERTY-DEFINITION ((*X)(FUZZY2 (INTENSITY *X) 30 50)))

*BRIGHT
(PROPERTY-DEFINITION ((*X)(FUZZY1 (INTENSITY *X) 25 45)))

*SHINING
(PROPERTY-DEFINITION ((*X)(FUZZY1 (BULE-VALUE *X) 50 60)))

*TEXTURAL
(PROPERTY-DEFINITION ((*X)(FUZZY1 (TEXTURE-DEGREE *X)
                                  1.0 4.0 (*BRIGHT *X))))
```

132

```
*HEAVY-TEXTURE
(PROPERTY-DEFINITION ((*X)(FUZZY1 (TEXTURE-DEGREE *X)
                                 5.0 7.0 (*BRIGHT *X))))
*GREY
(PROPERTY-DEFINITION ((*X)(FUZZY2 (SATURATION *X)
                                 0.05 0.15 (*BRIGHT *X))))
*VIVID
(PROPERTY-DEFINITION ((*X)(FUZZY1 (SATURATION *X)
                                 0.1 0.2 (*BRIGHT *X))))
*RED
(PROPERTY-DEFINITION ((*X)(FUZZY3H (HUE *X)
                                 5.0 5.5 0.1 0.6 (NOT (*GREY *X)))))
*BLUE
(PROPERTY-DEFINITION ((*X)(FUZZY3 (HUE *X)
                                 2.5 3.0 4.5 5.0 (NOT (*GREY *X)))))
*GREEN
(PROPERTY-DEFINITION ((*X)(FUZZY3 (HUE *X)
                                 0.5 1.0 2.5 3.0 (NOT (*GREY *X)))))
*YELLOW
(PROPERTY-DEFINITION ((*X)(FUZZY3H (HUE *X)
                                 5.8 0.0 1.0 1.5 (NOT (*GREY *X)))))
*HORIZONTALLY-LONG
(PROPERTY-DEFINITION ((*X)(FUZZY2 (VH-RATIO *X) -1.5 1.5)))

*VERTICALLY-LONG
(PROPERTY-DEFINITION ((*X)(FUZZY1 (VH-RATIO *X) -1.5 1.5)))

*MANYHOLE
(PROPERTY-DEFINITION ((*X)(FUZZY1 (HOLE-NUMBER *X) 0 10)))

*MANYLINE
(PROPERTY-DEFINITION ((*X)(FUZZY1 (LINE-DEGREE *X) 0.2 0.5)))

*HOLELINE
(PROPERTY-DEFINITION ((*X)(IF (GREATERP (HOLE-NUMBER *X) 2)
                          (FUZZY1 (HOLE-LINE-DEGREE *X) 0.2 0.5))))
*SAME-COLOR
(PROPERTY-DEFINITION
    ((*X *Y)(FUZZY2 (CROMATIC-DIFFERENCE *X *Y) 0.015 0.055)))

*WITH-IN
(PROPERTY-DEFINITION ((*X *Y)(FUZZY1 (O-RATIO *X *Y) 0.5 0.7)))

*WITH-IN2
(PROPERTY-DEFINITION ((*X *Y)(FUZZY1 (O-RATIO *X *Y) 0.0 0.1)))
```

```
*LINEAR-BOUNDARY
(PROPERTY-DEFINITION
    ((*X *Y)(IF (TOUCHING *X *Y)
            (FUZZY1 (BOUNDARY-LINE-DEGREE *X *Y) 0.2 0.5
                    (FUZZY1 (BOUNDARY-LENGTH *X *Y) 10 30)))))

*CONTACT
(PROPERTY-DEFINITION ((*X *Y)(T-RATIO *X *Y)))

*CONTACT2
(PROPERTY-DEFINITION ((*X *Y)(FUZZY1 (T-RATIO *X *Y) 0.1 0.3)))

*LOW-CONTRAST
(PROPERTY-DEFINITION
    ((*X *Y)(FUZZY2 (BOUNDARY-CONTRAST *X *Y) 1.0 2.0)))

*DARKER
(PROPERTY-DEFINITION
  ((*X *Y)(FUZZY1 (SUB (INTENSITY *Y)(INTENSITY *X)) -10 10)))

*W-RELATION
(PROPERTY-DEFINITION
    ((*X *Y)(IF (AND (NOT (IS *X *Y))(NOT (TOUCHING *X *Y)))
            (OR (AND (FUZZY3 (ANGLE-DIFFERENCE *X *Y 90)
                                        -30 -10 10 30)
                    (FUZZY3 (DISTANCE *X *Y)
                            0 (MULT (WIDTH-X *X) 2.0)
                            (MULT (WIDTH-X *X) 4.0)
                            (MULT (WIDTH-X *X) 6.0)))
                (AND (FUZZY3 (ANGLE-DIFFERENCE *X *Y
                            (OF SHAPE HL THETA *MRGN))
                        -45 -15 15 45)
                    (FUZZY3 (DISTANCE *X *Y)
                            0 (MULT (WIDTH-Y *X) 2.0)
                            (MULT (WIDTH-Y *X) 4.0)
                            (MULT (WIDTH-Y *X) 6.0)))))))))
```

NIL

Index

Procedural method, 4
Production rule, 91, 95
Production system, 4, 79, 91
Property, 58
   rule, 83

R-MERGE, R-CREATE(action), 96
Reconstruction
   color image, 36
   scene, 1
   segmented image, 69
Region, 75
   analysis, 2
   growing, 3
   merging, 3, 63
   segmentation, 2
   splitting, 3, 47
   sub-, 80
Relation, 66
   color, 61
   rule, 83
   topological, 61
Relaxation method, 90
Retrieval, 67
Rule, 82
   evaluation, 89
   if-done, 99
   to-do, 97
Rule-based, 4, 76

S-MERGE(action), 96
Scatter matrix, 61, 64
Scene, 80
   phase, 91
Scheduling, 94
Segmentation
   algorithm, 12, 47
   nonpurposive, 43
   over-, 33, 46
   preliminary, 43
   under-, 33
Semantic region analysis, 73
Symbolic representation of image, 46, 56

Task, 1
Task-specific knowledge, 43
Texture, 49